Bonnie & Barrey!
You already have a life you
love, you could write a better
book than this one I'm sure.

Create a Life You Love

Barrey. I study companies.
Yes, it starts from the top.
You created this amazing
culture with being who you are.
I was amazed the moment
I met you years ago in LV.
Thank you both for everything
2 b ~~~~~~~~ g to
will

Brooke :)

You already have a life you
love, you could write a bette-

# Create a Life You Love
## Reflections on Living Life to the Fullest

Reflections on Living Life to the Fullest

OZLEM BROOKE EROL

ISBN: 1507636822
ISBN 13: 9781507636824
Library of Congress Control Number: 2015900891
CreateSpace Independent Publishing Platform
North Charleston, South Carolina

Editing by Andrea Glass, www.WritersWay.com

*Dedicated to my only son, my husband, my parents, my brother, my extended family, my chosen family - my dear friends, and all the books and people who inspired me in my life. This book has something I learned from all of you. It wouldn't have been possible to write this without you being in my life. Thanks for all the gifts you have given me.*

# Table of Contents

# Acknowledgements

I want to thank my husband for supporting me in everything I do. I've always had your blessing, and only my own limitations and my fears kept me from doing this until now. I'm grateful.

I want to thank my son for making me a better person and understanding life in a much deeper sense. There's no better feeling in this world than being your mother. I'm so proud of the person you've become. I also wrote this book to inspire you to follow your dream. Don't listen to anyone (including me) but yourself. Always believe in yourself.

I can't offer enough thanks to my parents for teaching me how to be a caring human being with great values. You created the foundation of everything I've been able to achieve.

# A Special Thanks to People I've Never Met

I have to start with Oprah. Thank you Oprah, for being who you are, following your calling and teaching us about life every single day. I know it's no coincidence I found out about your show the first month I moved to the U.S. and I never stopped watching you or reading your *O Magazine*. You've changed my life and I'm grateful for that. You're one of the biggest influences in my life. One of my big dreams is to meet you in person one day.

Thank you to Eckhart Tolle for writing *New Earth*. That book made me understand the most important principles of spirituality.

Thank you to Gary Zukav, Mark Nepo, Brene Brown, Po Bronson, Marianne Williamson, Kristin Neff, Michael Singer, Martha Beck, Steven Pressfield, Howard Schultz and many others who have inspired me through their books and interviews.

Although I've never met any one of you, you've made a huge impact on me.

Thank you for shedding a light on so many people like me.

# Preface

This book was in me for a very long time. I've been writing since I was seven years old. I have diaries, notebooks, letters, articles and blogs. I always want to write. It's my therapy; it's my safe harbor; it's my outlet; it's the best way of expressing myself and the best tool to share what I learn. It's like a driving force in me, an energy that needs to get out. I just have to do it without being attached to any results.

Most important is I'm not different than any one of you. I don't claim to know everything. I'm not an expert in anything I share here. I'm a life-long learner and am practicing these life skills too. I have a passion to share what I've learned with any of you who want to read, who are curious, and who question life like I do. This book isn't intended to fix you. I hope you already have a great life but still want to be aware of some life skills to make it even better.

All the topics here are really about being human. All our flaws or weaknesses only make us more human, nothing else. There's really nothing "wrong" with any one of us. Some of what you read here may seem like common sense. What's common sense may not be common practice though, so you can make this a book of reminders. For some of you, the concepts and practices might not make too much sense. I don't ask you to agree or love everything I say. I can only kindly ask you to keep an open mind when you read it.

I don't know how to hold back what I've learned that has been useful and helpful in my life. If I can reach even a few people and make a positive impact in their lives with one thing I say in this book, I'll feel blessed.

I wish this book leaves you happier and/or more inspired about *your* life when you finish reading it. I'd like it to be your bedside book where you read one article at a time and feel better than when you started it. I sincerely wish some of what has helped me *to make the best out of my life and create a life I love* will bring some shine to yours too.

I'm so honored and thrilled that you're holding this book in your hands or in your e-reader right now! Thank you from the bottom of my heart. I would love to hear your thoughts about the book and what has stayed with you the most. You can email me at book@yourbestlifeinc.com.

And thank you to my relentless followers who have encouraged me to pull all my articles into one book. You've given me courage.

Love,
Ozlem Brooke Erol

# How to read this book

This book is mainly a collection of my blog articles and some other articles I've never shared before. You might see some repetitions in individual articles since they were all written at different times to reveal different concepts. At the same time, they're all related and some have common principles that are worth repeating.

The first part is about my journey and my story since everybody wants to know about the author. It is my version of Creating a Life I Love. The second part is mainly my articles about finding our purpose and following our dream. Since this is what I do on a daily basis for my coaching clients and I write quite often about this subject, the articles look and feel the same. They aren't meant to be read sequentially. Reading them in a row might not be the best idea because you'll see some repeated concepts in them, emphasizing the most important aspects of following our dream.

The rest of the articles discuss all the life skills I learned along the way that helped me make my life better and happier.

So you can either start reading from beginning to end or you can open up one page every day and only read one or two pieces. I see it as a bedside book to inspire you.

A few words about the language:

I want to feel like we're in a nice, casual conversation—you and I—rather than me lecturing you about a topic. Remember, it's sharing what I learned that I find valuable. I don't expect everyone to agree with everything I say. It's okay to disagree.

I use the term "Universe" throughout the book to be consistent. You can replace it with God, Higher Power, or any word you use based on your faith.

I use "soul" to mean everything we experience out of our physical body. It's the part of us connected to Universe/God/Oneness/Higher Self. That part of us that feels young even when we get old.

# My story

# My Journey

From a very young age, I always wanted to do something that touched people's lives in a meaningful and positive way. I had no idea how but it had to do with their daily lives, something that's directly linked to having a happier and more fulfilled life. I respect all jobs, all positions or all tasks equally (as long as it's not to destroy or harm humankind, nature or others for gaining power or money or for any selfish reason) because each of them makes this world a better place. I just feel we were all born to fill different roles. Even for the same roles, we all have a unique touch. This is the beauty. Most of us want the same things out of life no matter where we live or what we do. We have so many common traits and yet we all have unique gifts that make us special too. I love that we're born this way.

You have no idea how many times I questioned myself about writing this book all while having this intense urge to do it. Yet I thought about all the many talented writers who already wrote the best books on similar topics. Over time I understood that what comes from inside as a message or as a big energy—that little voice that tells you to do something over and over again—needs to be heard and we should all listen to it without thinking of the outcome. Like Nike says: We need to "Just do it".

But like many of us, life, family and society expectations carried me away from who I was and what I wanted to do. And I take full responsibility for straying; I have nobody but myself to blame. There are people who follow their bliss from very early on and walk through their own path no matter what the expectations are. I admire them a lot. I didn't spend too much time thinking about the platform I can use to achieve my goal of making people's lives a little better. I just remember a book my dad brought from the U.S. when I was a child that made a huge impact on me. It was Leo Buscaglia's book *Love*. I was so startled and excited to read he was giving classes on Love. I loved it. Can you really give classes on love? What a beautiful idea. I wanted to be like him. Everything in that book was impressive to me.

But as always I said, "He's a successful, intelligent man. He had a great education. He's very brave. He's special." So this kind of achievement belonged to him, not me. I was just a young girl in Turkey. Over the years I did this many times subconsciously: put others I admired on a higher pedestal. I was the weaker, the smaller and the less credible one. It's amazing how much suffering we can create for ourselves. Of course it took me decades before I even became aware of this inner talk that kept me small in some areas of my life.

# My Journey

As expected of me I did well in school. I went to one of the best middle and high schools in my hometown Istanbul, Turkey. It helped me to follow the path I was given because I was successful and success brought self-confidence with it every time I achieved the goals given to me. I was the May Queen in my senior year in high school where students and faculty choose someone who has good relationships and academics. I never thought about this until one of my coaches asked me to brag about some of the highlights of my life a few years back. When I was thinking about my younger years, I remembered this. It must have made me feel good at the time but it didn't make a big impact on me. I think it means more to me now knowing I was thought to be very humble. When the time came to decide on my major for college, I made decisions that I'm happy about to this day. I knew I wasn't going to like any technical field and that I wanted to stay close to social sciences. There were not many options at the time like I see for my son now. The most popular major in social sciences that was still kind of new in Turkey was Business Administration. So I worked enough to be in the top percentile as was expected from me to get into one of the best colleges in Turkey to get a degree that was very much sought after. It felt good. I loved the school and most of my classes; especially marketing which is related to human behavior, in my mind.

I want to pause here before I move forward and tell about a milestone during my college years. It happened when I was 20 years old. I even remember the day. I think I was already tired of trying to look good and saying the right things all the time to get approval from others. I made a conscious decision to be myself and not fake it. I remember I wanted to try this and see how it worked for me. I think that was an important moment in my life. I feel like I benefited from this decision throughout my life. I'm sure there are many moments where I still wanted to look good but for the most part I shared my ups and downs and to this day I feel like the reason so many people feel comfortable around me is that I give the same right to them—to be themselves. Not faking it, not trying to look like you know it all or act like I do the right things all the time. Yes I fail, yes I sometimes feel terrible, yes I make mistakes and it's okay. This was the first glimpse of being really authentic but I understood the depths of it years later.

I also had a great trip when I was 20 that changed my life. During my summer vacation, I took a trip to Italy with 60+ other young people from around the world. Thanks to the Lions Club International Youth Exchange Program. I thought if everybody had the same experience, the world would be a better place. I realized for the first time that we're all the same. Until then I learned about political differences we had with other countries and I thought we were significantly different from some other citizens of the world. I realized we were not. I loved the experience of it. That was the first time I thought of being a world citizen and I wanted to recreate that in my life; people from all walks of life from all different countries to live together peacefully, accepting our differences as something to celebrate.

Then without too much struggle—which was possible at that time after graduating from a good college—I got a job offer at IBM after many interviews and tests. Years later I found out all these achievements were great but they started to be part of my identity too. They served me well in many different aspects of my life but also served my ego more than my inner higher self.

I had excellent experiences and opportunities working for IBM. I got the best trainings there which I carried everywhere I went and I'm grateful for that. I met a lot of my best friends there. My gain was significant having worked there for 11 years.

However, no matter how great everything looked on paper, my inner voice was getting loud. In my 4th or 5th year, I had this strong feeling that I couldn't ignore the voice which said, "This isn't me. This isn't how I'm supposed to live my life." I started looking around. What else was I supposed to do? What could that job be? At the same time, I would see all my colleagues who were excited about what they did at IBM; I almost envied them. I wished I was like them. This was one of the best companies where you could work at the time. I made good money and the social life and the environment were great. I got to work with wonderful people. The company invested in their employees. So I felt bad and almost guilty to feel unfulfilled at a job many would love to have.

But my inner voice didn't stop. I didn't recognize it as my inner voice but I certainly heard it. As anybody who goes into conflict with her higher self, I became sick. I got ulcers. Lesson #1: Listen to your inner voice. Don't ignore it. You'll get sick if you don't do the right thing for yourself. At the time I knew it was stress related but I didn't exactly know how I caused it by betraying who I really was. I now know not only was I in conflict with who I really was, but I was trying to do things that were against my core values. I didn't know how values played such a big part in my life then. I couldn't explain this to myself or my family who believed I had the perfect job. After my journey of 15 years with my true self now, I know why I had this major inner turbulence; but it wasn't so easy to articulate it at the time.

Thankfully the Universe helped me. I had the perfect excuse. I had this opportunity to move to the U.S. with my family because we won the green card lottery. I had this dream of living in the U.S. since I was a child and it was happening. Also my experience in Italy had a big impact on me. I wanted to live somewhere with diversity.

So I quit my "perfect" job. I knew I had to do it. When I look back I see that after every self-betrayal, life again and again found a way to stop me from doing something that was killing my soul. In every case I always heard my inner/higher self-voice yet I always found good reasons to ignore it, not to leave the job that didn't serve me well. It happened every time. Sometimes I couldn't do it myself; I had to be laid off so I could reclaim my soul. I'm amazed and also

# My Journey

grateful to the Universe to come to my rescue each time even though it didn't feel so great at those very moments.

Moving to the U.S. was major for me and my husband. We had to leave everything familiar behind—our wonderful families, great network of friends and a good financial standing—and step into a lot of unknowns. I sometimes think of that time and wonder how we ever found the courage to make this huge move. We took the biggest risk of our lives and I wish I remembered it more often when I judge myself for not being brave enough! It was a search for a better life and I think this is a drive I carry around all the time. I believe we're a little different than our parents' generation in terms of tolerating and questioning. Some of them were more conservative for the most part and lived through life accepting many things as they were. We question everything. Our career, our relationships, having a child, choosing where to live, our health—everything. Having the opportunity to travel a lot and experiencing the western world, both my husband and I were eager to raise our son in a more civilized environment with more choices than we had in Turkey. We loved our country but it always felt difficult to live there with the values we were brought up with. We especially didn't know which values and virtues we wanted to raise our son with so he could be happy and also adapt well to his native country.

People still ask me why we made the move. And the best answer is "our intuition told us so to do so". I always try to find the best answers based on who's asking so it sounds right but it never works. If I'm able to give the right answer I would be called crazy. We were crazy to leave everything behind but especially our great jobs and financial status. We were crazy to go to the unknown with only our savings. We were crazy to start all over as a family in the other part of the world. I think to this day it really is crazy and it takes crazy people to do it. But it was a force from within and we had to do it no matter what. It's very hard to explain it to logical people who live a straight forward life. I love that my husband turned out to be as crazy as I'm! (And we all know this country is made up of many more "crazy" people like us.)

People in California where we chose to live were very welcoming. There are people from all around the world here and I appreciate this environment a lot. I feel like I can live with my values here.

The first job I took in the U.S. as a Project Manager was completed in 2002. I was looking for the next job to pay our bills. Then somebody came into my life who forced me to ask the hardest questions to myself. "What do I REALLY want to do? What do I love? What are my strengths?" That process was the most meaningful thing I did for myself. It was the most precious time I spent for my own good. Understand that it didn't feel like bliss all the time though. I wasn't making money at first and I had no idea what to do next. I felt unsuccessful and like I was wasting a lot of time. Like Steve Jobs says, "You can't connect the dots looking forward; you can only connect them looking backwards. So you have to trust that the dots will somehow connect in your future." You don't understand why things happen when they do. But now I do.

I had a few coaches who helped me during that process and it changed my life. I remember how I felt excited to find out what I wanted to do and that some of what I already knew was all verified. I was very excited waiting to conquer the world. I remember it so well. That was when I started my coaching business. I thought I can help anyone interested to find their passion, their unique gifts so they could live their own best lives. I couldn't think of anyone who wouldn't want to go through this process. What's more important than finding out what you love to— besides to love and be loved? (I was wrong. I met many people who never want to go through this journey for many different reasons which I'll point out throughout the book.) As far as we know we have this short life on earth so why not make the most out of it? Why sell our soul to something we hate to do?

I always had faith that the Universe always had faith that the Universe is available to help you out and make miracles. I had my is available to help you out and make miracles. I had my doubts nevertheless. I wanted to believe so bad but fear always caught up with me. I got that I was raised to excel and I expected not to "fail" at all, whatever that meant in my mind. Well coming to a new country where none of your credentials mean a thing, you kind of fall flat on your face. You face your ego. Stripped away from a lot of identities I captured subconsciously along the way in Turkey, I had to look deeper inside to understand who I really was besides my titles (not only work but social labels as well). My ego got a lot of bruises for sure but it helped me understand myself better. For the first time in my life, I felt like I was "failing" with my made-up definition of who I was supposed to be. I was "not having a stable and secure life" like I created back in Turkey. Unfortunately coming from a self-judgmental place I was the one failing. It wasn't a failure outside of my body; it was a part of me. This is when it gets downhill for anyone; when we take it too personally. Now I know having read stories of people I admire, failing, making mistakes and not knowing what the next step will look like are parts of playing big. You risk everything by leaving everything familiar behind or by starting a new venture or by sharing your creative piece. You'll not always feel like you're in control. It's going to be scary but it's worth it. The ones who persist are the ones who don't take failing personally and get up and do it all over again. They know *"what they tried* failed", and it's not them who failed as a person. They know this is part of life especially if you want to create a life you love. I know it and believe it now but there was some self-suffering until I learned this.

So even though I started my first business in 2003 and was very excited about it, there were a lot of other challenges I had to face. Those of you who have your own businesses may relate to some of this. I understood very fast that having your own business required a whole different mindset which

I didn't have at the time. Having sold millions of dollars of hardware to customers without the blink of an eye, there I was in front of my own prospects speechless when they asked me how much I charged for my services. Knowing exactly how priceless it is to help people transform their lives to live their passion, I still couldn't ask for money for what I did. Then I had to look at all my issues around money. I wasn't aware of them until I was forced to look into them. Like all of us I had my blind spots. We don't know what we don't know. I had to work on this issue for years. I feel like besides having a child, having your own business is one of the biggest milestones in life where you need to recognize your issues that need to be resolved. I had way too many questions. It was overwhelming. "Who was I to do this? What was my credibility? Who am I to call myself a coach? Why would anyone ever hire me?" But I never blinked an eye to pay high amounts when I believed in another coach. Over the years I learned nobody really cared about my credentials but only who I was being. How I showed up to help them.

So I prayed to have a normal job to pay my bills and although I pursued my passion for coaching it stayed mostly in the background. I did a lot of pro-bono coaching which helped me tremendously but my mind told me I had to be logical and use my years of experience in sales and marketing. Then I found a job at a local company. Good. A big relief. What was that "owning your business" all about? Whew! I can do it as a hobby on the side. (That's the sound of selling myself and staying small!)

Years went by. I felt peaceful most of the time. I liked the people I worked with which is very important to me. I gave my heart and soul to this company from the smallest office decisions to the big ones. I was heavily invested. I liked the fact that I had a big impact and was able to contribute a lot unlike working for a larger company. I felt appreciated. When I look back now it's interesting how much I needed the appreciation at the time. All the good things I didn't tell myself were expressed and that meant a lot to me. Lesson #2: If you know your own value and tell yourself all the things you deserve, you don't need anybody else's approval or appreciation. At some point I knew I wasn't gaining anything anymore and I knew I could do better than this job I had. My inner/higher voice was getting louder again but I had gotten too comfortable and found good excuses not to leave. I didn't quit when I knew it was the right thing to do. (How many times do we pretend not to hear our gut? It's never served me well not to listen to it.)

The Universe was watching and saw me not feeding my soul again. "Here you go; she's not going to do what's best for her on her own. I need to send her a message again." I got laid off after seven years when recession hit our company. I was expecting it but I didn't take charge of my life on my own. Lesson #3: Don't sell your soul! Listen to your inner voice. You know when the time is right or what's best for you. Listen and do it.

The next day I started looking for a new job. I had to. We had bills to pay. I tortured myself in the process. No breaks, no going back to Turkey to see the family when I had a chance to do it without getting permission from anyone. Of course not. You have to work! We were in the middle of recession. So I found another job. In the 2nd interview I knew it wasn't the right job for me. But no job in a recession. My mind said. "Take it anyway." It was bad even during my first week. All the things I don't believe in had to be done. That "Selling my soul" song was playing again. I was a lot more aware this time though so it was even more unbearable. I was glad to have nice people around me but what was I supposed to do there? I told myself to look at the bright side, find positive things. Please. Then I got a chance for another position in the same company and I took it. This was better but still I knew this wasn't it. I was too responsible to quit my job. I needed to pay the bills. But here it came, that same voice: "Here she is again. She's going to really harm herself if she keeps on doing this." And they closed my department altogether. Lesson #4. When you know right from the start something isn't good for you, don't even start. Don't say yes. Don't sell your soul. Don't act with fear. The good part: I wasn't even surprised this time. I definitely didn't take it personally. I stayed there for the last day and said my good-byes. I took my personal stuff which was very little this time (I learned not to make it my own personal space this time) and left. I never looked back.

This time I took the message seriously. At least partly I should say. My longing to be my own boss since 2003 had to come true this time. I started my marketing company then. Enough is enough. Did I learn something out of all these experiences? Of course. They all happened to teach me something about myself. This is how we grow. Since that day I've been working hard for my business to be successful. I also realized that doing marketing and doing passion/career coaching have a lot in common: I want to bring out the best in people or the best in companies. I primarily do the same thing in both of my businesses. Now I am slowly transitioning to helping companies do the right thing, move away from the dehumanizing part of business and being honest and still making great profit. Companies who value their people, who look at them as human beings instead of numbers and machines. This is a very exciting time for people like me who wanted to see the change.

During this whole journey, even though I had difficult times, I always felt happy. I always had good things happening to me. I always loved my life here. I had many great stories and celebrations. I got lucky to meet amazing people in this far-away county. I'm truly blessed. But the purpose of this story is to share my lessons of life. As is true for many of us most lessons come through difficult experiences, so that's what I share.

When I switch from what's logical and looks good on paper to speaking from my truth and from my strong higher self, life always gets better. Whenever I stray from my path, the Universe has no pity for me anymore. I know I'll face even more challenges if I do things only out of my logical mind. My intuition and my heart always have to be part of the process; they don't make mistakes as much as my rational mind does.

I'm working on myself, on my business, on my fears on a daily basis. It's an unbelievable journey. I don't think it's ever going to end. I'm finding out I'm a big fighter inside and I always believe in good things. As human beings we're very complicated yet very simple. I'm 100% sure we create most of our suffering and our beliefs. We never question them but they're the only limiting factors to achieving what we want. Now I know there's a way out.

My goal continues to be to learn how to make the best out of this life with the elimination of superficial worries, made-up stories, limiting beliefs and blind spots. I want to take an active role in my life and make sure nothing artificial stops me from living the best version of it. And I'll continue to share all I learn along the way.

*"Walk with the dreamers, the believers, the courageous, the cheerful, the planners, the doers, the successful people with their heads in the clouds and their feet on the ground. Let their spirit ignite a fire within you to leave this world better than you found it."*

— WILFRED PETERSON

# About Writing

I've always loved writing. It has been my best friend, my therapy, my outlet, my survival instinct in this world. I had to share my experiences; my notebooks, my diaries and then my laptop were always there for me. Something almost constantly forced me to write. I had this urge to share what I know and what I learn. I know people around me aren't always ready to hear what I have to say but I have to share it anyway. I never wrote with an intention to do something about it; I just HAD to write. I think I like to talk and speak as much as I like to write; you don't have a chance to speak to people as often though but you can write anytime and anywhere. It also gives people a choice— only the ones interested will buy the book and read it. When you speak not everybody is willing to listen. Writing saves my life. I don't know how to live without it.

The earliest writings I found are from a dairy I started when I was seven. Years ago I found it and laughed so much about the details I shared in my notebooks. I loved to see what was significant then.

The biggest milestone was sending one of my articles to a newspaper without letting anybody know about it and when it got published in a book with other young writers' pieces, I was very happy. I was proud of being published for the first time.

In my adult years I always wrote one thing or another. I have several notebooks; in some I take notes during trips, in some I jot down life tips and in others I have thoughts from books and authors. I keep a notebook for my son and one gratefulness journal. I also had a few more short articles that got published in newspapers.

Then in 2002 I created my own website to write and bring together all the articles that moved and inspired me. Here I was online. When you want to do something you can't live without, you get really creative.

Blogs came into being; what a neat idea. I already had my website to write my articles but this was another great tool for me to continue sharing. I loved to learn but the pace expanded exponentially after I moved to the U.S. I was out of the box and with my thirst to learn I started reading even more, watching and observing everything in my new environment—which meant I had even more to write about. I also found Oprah (I'm sure by no coincidence; when you're open, inspiring people appear in your life and there are few who've had such a huge impact on me like Oprah—at least among all the people I've never met). Every time I watched Oprah my muse got activated.

Something that also inspired me happened in 2013. I wrote a letter to a group of people I'd never met and posted it on Facebook. I remember that exact day and where I was when I wrote it. I was at a friend's house talking about business. In the meantime I was reading some of the events that were unfolding in my home country. I got very emotional and wanted to respond to some young protestors in my hometown of Istanbul. On my way home I knew I wasn't able to wait to write until I get there. With an indescribable pull I felt inside, I stopped and sat down at a café shop I loved and wrote the letter and posted it on Facebook hoping it would reach the people I intended it for. And a miracle happened as they describe in books I've read about angels helping out of the blue when you want something so badly. A dear high school friend whom I had not seen for 20+ years saw the post and made print outs to take to those young protestors. I was in awe of this happening one day after I posted the letter! I'm so grateful to my friend for taking this on. Then a few days later some other friend in San Diego mentioned my name in Facebook and when I looked at it, it was the video of someone reading my letter out loud to the crowd I intended to reach back in Istanbul. And the person who taped it happened to be a friend I had not seen for 15+ years from IBM. He posted the video on Facebook. He said some people had tears in their eyes when my letter was read to them. How can you explain this? Like Steven Pressfield and many others I've read and listened to for all these years have said: Your angels line up when you're doing what you're supposed to do and when you act from your heart. When you know you have to do something and don't have any idea how to do it but just do it anyway, things work out in an amazing way. When I think back I can recall similar experiences. I shared this one because it has to do with my writing. The bottom line is whatever dream I had that I believed in happened. All those that I thought were a little bit too much or too good for me to dream didn't. This is true.

With everything I learned I was even more drawn to my calling; sharing my writing or speaking and helping anyone who wanted to find the answers to a more fulfilled life. So I kept on writing. I knew from the bottom of my heart that I wanted to write my book; something about living a better or a more extraordinary life. I don't know the title of the book as I write these lines but for the first time I know for sure it's going to happen. Although I always wrote one thing or another I procrastinated on actually starting to write the book. I felt this crazy self-sabotaging force of energy that kept me from going to my desk. This is real. It was a strong energy I felt every time I wanted to start writing my book even when some of the pieces were already there. It sounds crazy but after reading a lot of stories about writers, artists and business owners I knew I wasn't alone. What made me sit down and write everything I was carrying in my head was Steven Pressfield's book *The War of Art*. This book really helped me understand what was happening to me all these years. How can you not start doing what you know for sure you have to do? I always knew it. It's impossible not to hear the voice especially after practicing years and years in self-discovery and self-awareness. Yet I still didn't do it. Amazing stuff about human beings. The best explanation was found in his book; Resistance! It's like a universal law. When you're up to something big that will elevate your soul or help others, resistance is automatically there. You can't miss it. The higher the calling the larger the resistance, he says. Pressfield explains how common this is among writers and artists. I was so relieved to hear this. It explained a lot for me.

I've always loved books. They've changed my life. I started being interested in books when I was in kindergarten in Boston when my family lived there for two years. I remember short moments at the library. Even at a young age, being at the library and in the presence of so many books shifted something in me. Then my middle school and high school libraries were a treasure for me. I had summer vacations when I would read the whole series of books of a certain publisher. I don't have enough time to experience different lives and places so books give me the privilege to do that. Half of who I'm is made up of the books I read both fiction and non-fiction. I never ever get bored when I'm waiting at an airport or waiting for anyone who's late if I have a book with me. I'm one of those people who feel the happiest in a bookstore or in a library totally taken away by the smell and presence of books. It's hard to describe the joy I feel when I'm around books. So creating a book of my own is very special to me. If I was to die today and was asked "What do you regret?" I would say, "Not having written my book." So it had to be done.

I have no idea how well this book will be received. But I have to publish it. I want to take my hand over the cover and feel it. I want to smell the pages. Although this may turn into a digital book I have to have a printed one. I understand the benefits of digital publishing and I'm one of those people open to new things but I love, love, love books I can hold in my hands and smell.

I just wanted to tell you about this strong powerful voice inside me that told me to write no matter what. The reason I bring it up and will do again in this book is to hopefully inspire you, to move you to do the same for your own calling whatever it might be. To hear your higher self's voice. Not the one that depends on your survival and material things (the voice of your ego which wants you to stay small and to be safe) but the other one—the voice coming from a higher energy, your most sacred part, your real self. Do it. One of my goals is to take you out of that place of self-doubt and make you a believer in yourself and your talents and your inner unbreakable power.

Happy "writing"—whatever that might be in your life.

# All about our purpose and passion in life

*"Your work is going to fill a large part of your life, and the only way to be truly satisfied is to do what you believe is great work. And the only way to do great work is to love what you do."*

— STEVE JOBS

# CONNECTION BETWEEN PASSION AND AWARENESS

I believe we come to this planet for a reason. We all have a purpose for being here. We probably know it best when we were a child. Then real life kicks in with school, grades and expectations of parents and society. Since we're all programmed to receive love, we pick and choose what we do by the reaction and love we get from the people we care about. We would do anything to get that loving smile from our parents. We lose ourselves somewhere during that process of growing up. I'm in awe of people who don't fall off their path and follow it no matter what others say or think. That to me is a great indication of their faith in who they're.

For most of us though, it's either a question that never comes up again or a very difficult one to manage if it does. Why am I here? What am I supposed to do with my life? It's easy to ignore since we have a lot of obligations by the time we have a job and a family. The bottom line always comes to: "I have to pay the bills and I'm not going to dwell on these big questions." "I don't have time for it." "Only dreamers go there." That makes sense logically, however, when I hear and learn about successful (success meaning they love what they do and feel happy) people, almost all of them followed their dream no matter what. When they come forward, they tell how they listened to their heart's desire. They never say it's a smooth ride either but at the end they feel more fulfilled than people who only work to "make a living". I think it's worth looking into these deep questions since we all want to feel happy most of the time in this short life we live. It doesn't need to be a big career change either; we just need to identify what makes us feel excited and then learn how to integrate it into our lives.

Many people ask me how to find their passion and their purpose when I tell them I do coaching in this area. I hear, read and observe over and over again from everybody who's able to clarify their passion that the only way to hear that inner voice is to increase our awareness level. Paying attention to what we do, how we feel, what makes us excited, what's calling us, being in the moment—all help us answer these questions. Practicing stillness is the gateway to our awareness. Happy people swear by the power of meditating, taking time to be in nature and being free of the chatter in our mind—even for brief moments—as a means of increasing self-awareness. The answers are within. We just need to get reconnected to that place that exists inside us and knows why we're here and what we're supposed to do with our lives. I wish happy awareness and stillness for everyone!

*"You have to make sure your dream is inextricably linked to who you are."*

— AMA YAWSON

# Resistance to do what you love

I've been struggling with this for a long time now. Every time I'm up to something big, I love to make the plans and have the dream but I have this big resisting energy right before I do something about it. It doesn't make any sense logically. What makes sense is to start what you love to do right away just like the Nike tagline says "Just do it". So where does this resistance to act come from? I can never explain it. It definitely feels like self-sabotage. You know your soul wants it, you know it carries a lot of meaning for you, yet you don't start doing it.

I told the story at the beginning of the book about my journey but for those who skipped that part, here's a reminder. I listened to an interview with Steve Pressfield. He believes that when we're up to something big for ourselves or for others, the resistance is there automatically. It's almost like a universal law. Then I bought his book *The War of Art* and read more about it. It's so interesting the way he describes it, feeling so familiar and making me feel a little less crazy. It looks like many people go through this phase. I had that feeling of "Thank God I'm not the only one. May be I don't need to beat myself up; there's a reason behind my insanity." He says the more important the task or the dream, the bigger the resistance. That's so true. I start the steps to achieve a lot of things I want but not the steps to my biggest calling.

It could be running your first marathon, pursuing your dream of becoming a painter, writing your book or starting a new venture. The more you want it, harder it is to start this journey.

The best thing to realize is there's hope. There are ways to get around the resistance and do what we love anyway. We actually all know in our guts that this calling will bring us joy and feed our soul; we just have to recognize resistance for what it is and start our unique journey to be who really are and share our form of "art". I'll leave the secrets to overcoming it to Pressfield's great book. At this time I just wanted you to recognize that if you're up to something important and feel the resistance, you can relax—you're not the only one and there are ways to overcome it.

*"The two most important days in your life are the day you're born and the day you find out why."*

— MARK TWAIN

# Living self-aware, listening to your inner voice

I think I lived a long time being unconscious. I always knew what I was doing but not what was behind it or what was driving my actions. Now I hear my "little voice" all the time and I can thank her for her advice and still move on. It's important to understand that *mean* voice is there to protect us; sometimes it works in our favor but mostly it wants us to stay small and be safe. Being safe is good when we're up against danger but not when it stops us from doing what we want. Some call it the saboteur, some call it the devil voice, and some call it our ego. Basically it's that voice that tells us we cannot do it. The voice that's not so gentle and mostly judging.

The other whisper we can hear—if we pay attention of course—is so much better though. It's the *real* you. The real you isn't in your mind but in your body or your heart as sensations or feelings. You know deep down it feels right; it feels like the real you. If you can silence that ego's little voice there's so much hope, love and creativity in there. It may not always look so logical or rational because it's not in your mind. You just know it without knowing how you know it, as Martha Beck (coach and writer) says. It's your intuition. As human beings we were so much more in tune with who we were in the past. Now with our super busy lives we don't hear ourselves. We literally lost ourselves. We're almost always in auto-pilot mode, that is until we practice more awareness.

Do you know how I got to be in tune with myself? The first 30 years of my life my little voice dictated everything. Did it work for me? Yes. In many ways. But when I started to pay attention to the soft whispers (the gentler voice of my real self) they started getting louder than the ego's voice. Although everything about my life looked great on the out-side I was looking for something missing in my life—on the inside. I wasn't sure what it was but I knew at least what I didn't want. When I finally decided to quit my job and re-ally listened to what my heart was saying and took the risk against every logical explanation and moved to the U.S. to start over again, things started to shift. I'm not saying it was easy. It wasn't; but something inside me told me this was what I needed to do. I listened. When I got out of the cor-porate world and came into a different environment I was able to recharge. I know the biggest trick was to make time for myself to stay still. Then over the years I learned about meditation. The biggest benefit of it is to silence your mind even if for only a minute. Then you can add more time as you reconnect to who you really are. We're still in there somewhere. We didn't leave our bodies but we just haven't been listening. We hear all the chatter around us but not the gentle voice that tells us what's right for us to make us happy and fulfilled.

It's still sometimes a struggle for me. I'm not there every day and certainly not every minute but I'm building this muscle. As I do more, I hear more of who I really am and it feels great. Then I can listen to it wherever I am. At home, at work, with my friends—everywhere. Even though some thoughts are really scary I know deep down that listening to my inner voice is where I need to be. It gives me a chance to stop for a second and act differently. I question if what I tell myself is the truth or if I'm making it all up. It stops me from going into my drama. It's really one of the best life skills I've learned which has had a positive impact on every aspect of my life.

I usually take the harder path and I'm willing to do the work. You may not want to go there with me. However the alternative is scarier I guess: where I made up stories that weren't true, where I only reacted to life but didn't create it and where I had lots of regrets at the end. I'd rather be disappointed than have a lot of regrets; at least I know I tried.

*"There's no passion to be found playing small – in settling for a life that's less than the one you're capable of living."*

— NELSON MANDELA

# Staying "small"

ooking at children I always think how everything is possible at their young age. All dreams are big and exciting. This is before family's and society's expectations and norms take over. Then we start to look like many others. We lose the connection to our powerful self. We seek so much approval and love from people around us that we'll change or do anything to make them happy. It's so nice to feel "approved of" when we meet the expectations of our parents or society. We don't necessarily feel very excited about our life but we must be on the right track since we don't feel judged so much. We made it in this world. If we ever think big there are many people—including our parents—who remind us we may fail or we may be disappointed and we need to choose a safe path. For most of us in my generation, the formula is: Go to a good school, find a good job, and be nice.

So this gets us to stay in our mind most of the time. We start to be really logical. We stop paying attention to what our hearts and our guts say—where all creation resides. We start making smaller dreams. Just to be safe. We don't want to fail. We have to meet expectations. Subconsciously we're afraid to lose the love we receive if we do something not expected of us. God forbid if we try something out of the ordinary and we fail. We think we'll probably be abandoned.

We arrive at middle age without even putting any thought into important questions like what makes us happy, what our calling is, what we want our legacy to be. We have an ordinary life which is okay. However, some of us start to hear our powerful self again around this time especially if we have a job we don't like, we don't have a life partner we love or we feel like our life doesn't carry any significance. We may start to look for more meaning in our life. We may even get to see our gifts more clearly than ever. Then comes the second hard part: to step into your real self again. Somewhere deep inside we know we have more potential but it's so hard to be as brave as we were in our childhood. What if we fail as an adult? What if these questions are only for the lucky ones who have a lot of money to pursue their dreams? What if we lose what we already have? It's so much easier to stay small and be in our comfort zone. We already adapted a way of being all these years. Even if we feel bad sometimes we're used to having those feelings. How am I supposed to adapt to these new feelings of having 100% faith in myself and feeling really excited as I did as a child? We know it may feel good but it's also very scary as an adult.

Unfortunately most of us stop there. We decide to live a good ordinary life (or a really miserable one because now we hear our higher self even louder telling us our calling). It's really okay to live this life and we shouldn't make ourselves wrong for it. Most people in the world live like this.

I'm just inviting you for a minute to think differently. Think about your big dream and imagine how you would feel if you could achieve this. Visualize it. How much more joy and freedom would you have to express who you really are and to share your uniqueness and gifts with the world? What's the impact of not realizing this dream you care about? Having worked with very brave clients I know there's a possibility for everyone to have their dreams come true. Our excuses not to follow them are usually not right. They're based on survival and our ego. It's our fear. We have to stop staying small and hiding our gifts from the world. Everything around you, big and small, started with somebody's dream. What if they had decided not to share that with us?

There's a way to live an extraordinary life and play BIG if you choose to do so!

*"Your time is limited, so don't waste it living someone else's life. Don't be trapped by dogma, which is living with the results of other people's thinking. Don't let the noise of others' opinions drown out your own inner voice. And most important, have the courage to follow your heart and intuition."*

— STEVE JOBS

# Music Within

recently watched a movie about a man named Dr. Richard Pimentel who prepared the Disability Act which passed in 1990 in the U.S. It enables people with disabilities to work. Shocking that it was so recent. A little over two decades ago! The movie *Music Within* showed that because those with disabilities made others uncomfortable they were kicked out of a restaurant. The restaurant had the right to do that before this law passed. Unbelievable!

But the story was about Richard who had a teacher that encouraged adults with disabilities to find their own music within. Richard made a big difference for many others because he followed something that was important for him. He decided to stand up for this cause.

I believe we all come here with a purpose and I think we have an obligation to find out what it is. It doesn't have to be big or earth shattering but it has to be about sharing something we have to offer the world. It could be touching a few people's lives by being there for them; it could be to invent something; it could be to serve people by selling something you truly believe in; it could be anything you do with passion knowing it's your calling.

What I'm most passionate about is for people to find their calling! There's no better use of your time than finding out why you're here. It's so amazing that we all have our unique qualities and talents that we bring to this world.

Some of us find ourselves in our 30s or 40s or even later in life. The answers are not out there.  They're already in you. You want to know how to find it? Just listen to why you're here in whispers first and then what comes as obvious to you. Pay attention to your strengths, what people tell you, what makes you feel like the real you, what makes you excited and juiced up more than anything. Or hire a coach to help you with that! Nothing can be more worth your time and money to find out! You certainly will enjoy your life and be happier once you discover the real you!

*"If you're not afraid of your dreams,
your dreams aren't big enough"*

— A<small>NONYMOUS</small>

# POTENTIAL

As I learn more about the science behind our minds and our soul, my feelings are of excitement for the future of humanity on one hand and sadness for many lives wasted because they not aware of their potential on the other hand.

We're all born with an amazing amount of energy to create. We all bring great gifts. We all believe in big dreams, that everything is possible. Then education, society and others' expectations kill our soul little by little—unless we were lucky enough to grow up in an environment where being yourself and following your own path is encouraged.

We start to play so safe, so small that we lose all our power. Our thinking becomes limited and we don't even know it. All those limited beliefs seem so real. We build many blind spots and start to live in small restrained spaces that we create. We stop believing in ourselves and that anything is possible. Once we lose the connection to our powerful higher self—our soul—life becomes more predictable. We start to feel more comfortable in this limited life we created since it becomes familiar. We don't want to take risks and look bad if we fail. We even get irritated by people who are playing big and having extraordinary lives. Or we admire them and believe they're special and more powerful than we are while we bury the same capacity and potential in ourselves.

But when we look at people who do use their potential and share their gifts, we know we benefit from them. We wouldn't have a lot of advancements in our lives or material things around us if people who dreamed about them never made it happen just to be safe and stay small. It's almost unfair not to share what we know—our talents, our gifts—because we keep people from enjoying them as well. It could be our love, a painting, a piece of music, a new technology, an article, a delicious food—anything! Nothing is insignificant; one song can make us feel so good, a painting can take us on an inner journey, a piece of new technology can connect us with our loved ones, a delicious dish can make us feel all our senses, showing extra care and love to someone can change his/her life forever. Whatever is in you that makes you feel great, do it and share it so we can all have a better world to live in. Let's not waste our potential to stay safe or because we're so afraid to fail. Then we can all stop being sad and get excited about the future of our planet where everybody gets to share their gifts.

*"It's never too late to be what you might have been."*

— GEORGE ELIOT

# What stops us?

As I take more responsibility for my life I see that the things that happened or didn't happen to me are products of my own decisions. When I say I really want something and don't do anything to get it, I see that the stories I make up or the blaming I do are defense mechanisms. That helps me stay in the comfort zone even though I may not like it at all. We get so used to our comfort zone, it's amazing. We see the right to complain and whine about what we don't have but we don't do enough to change it. It's as if we want to get negative attention with our whining. Do we really want to change our circumstances or is it more comfortable to complain, blame and stay where we are? Is complaining done to cover up our fear of moving forward with our dreams? Do we want to make our excuses so real so nobody keeps us accountable to follow our path?

I'm so guilty of this. I remember my first job and how I started to feel out of place there. Instead of taking the necessary actions to change it or at least accept what I had until I could move on, all I did was complain and whine. I feel bad when I think of my coworkers at the time. If any of you are reading this now, I want to apologize. I'm in awe that you were so patient with me. I still can't believe none of you said, "If you're so unhappy, leave us alone and go. Quit complaining so much. Don't stay and keep whining. This is crazy." That's what I needed to hear but everybody around me was too kind to say that. I kept torturing myself and others for years.

It's very clear to me that we're our worst enemy when it comes to following our big dreams. We listen to our limiting little voice and stop ourselves from becoming who we were meant to be. Think of someone who you love, what they bring to the world. For example, if you love Starbucks, think of Howard Schultz and his dream; or the little bakery shop around the corner; or the author who changed your life; or Dalai Lama who spent his life for more peace; or the brain surgeon who saved your niece's life. Now think of those people staying hidden and not sharing their gifts with the world. It's the same with each of us. We all have something to share with the people around us. It doesn't have to make headlines in the most popular newspaper but if we can all touch one more person's life with our gifts that will change the world one person at a time.

Next time you come up with excuses and stories about why you can't follow your dream stop and ask yourself this question: Am I being true to myself? Is this a real reason or the easy way out to stay in my comfort zone? What you're facing might be a relevant reason but think if you can overcome it and make your dream come true sometime in the near future.  At least be brave enough to tell the truth to yourself; it will change you and how you perceive life.

This isn't about making ourselves guilty but about being authentic to ourselves. There's no right or wrong answer. We can all take responsibility for what we're willing to do and be okay with it. Let's all say NO to stopping ourselves.

*"One of the most courageous things you can do is to identify yourself, know who you are, what you believe in and where you want to go."*

— SHEILA MURRAY BETHEL

# WHO ARE YOU?

**W**e rarely ask that question of ourselves. And if we do, the answers are related to what we do: our job title usually comes first. Then if we think thoroughly the next few things will be our different roles in life: mother, sister, daughter, father, son, granddaughter, cousin or friend. But we rarely sit down and think about who we are. I know you may be wondering what I'm talking about because we're not usually asked this question. We decide who we are by deciding *who we want to be* right now. Do you want to be a loving person no matter what? Do you want to be unstoppable no matter what life throws at you? Do you want to be a contribution, compassion or an inspiration for others? Who are you being? How do people see you?

You can decide for yourself at this moment and live that life from now on! You can be conscious of who you are whatever situation you may be in. If you create yourself as a compassionate person, see if you can be "compassion" where there's hatred or wrong-doing. The biggest element of being who you declare to be is to be in integrity with it. Your actions should also show who you are. You need to walk the talk. I met a great leader once who is in integrity with who she claims to be. She chose to help people live an extraordinary life. Everything she does is in alignment with this. She walks the talk all the time. That doesn't mean she never has times when she may not want to act like it but she reminds herself each time who she really is. Not her ego, not her title, not her past stories—but her real essence in this world. I'm inspired by people like that.

Think of Martin Luther King, Steve Jobs, Gandhi or Maya Angelou. They weren't about their title, they were about what they stood for. We all know it when we see these types of people.

Do this exercise: write down who you are without the titles and roles you hold. What is it that your heart really desires for you and the world around you? Think about what makes you different from others. Think about what comes natural to you. If you can't uncover it, you can just declare who you are right now. Then embrace it, feel it and remember it in everyday life. Be fully self-expressed from a place of who you truly are. You'll feel great I promise.

Do you want to know who I really am? I am a stand for people to discover their gifts and potential and to live them. It doesn't matter how I do it or which platforms I use; behind everything I do I want to be that person. And I always have the right to change my path and make it even better!

*"I never made one of my
discoveries through the process
of rational thinking."*

— ALBERT EINSTEIN

## Finding your passion isn't a fluffy empty statement

I've always been drawn to positive quotes like "Dream big", "The future belongs to those who dream" and many others I now share on my Facebook page and Twitter account. Although I loved reading about them one part of me was suspicious. It sounded too good to be true. So to feel good I surrounded myself with these quotes but I never looked deep down into the reality of these statements said by very smart people.

Being attracted to understanding people's potential, their gifts and their passion made me look into the stories of people I admired. In all their sharing, I started hearing the same message over and over. Howard Schultz of Starbucks, John Mackey, co-founder of Whole Foods, Oprah Winfrey, Deepak Chopra, Steve Jobs, Albert Einstein, Vincent van Gogh, Paul Coelho and many others from all walks of life say the same thing: Listen to your heart, pay attention to those gifts you bring and do what you love—and the rest will follow.

So I recommend you read the stories of these incredible people, if you're skeptical. Reading about them made me believe more in these "fluffy" sentences. These weren't about empty promises but brave actions of people who chose to follow their paths.

You and I'll still get a lot of resistance from the people around us when we step into our dreams unless we're surrounded with people who are open and believe in these same concepts. If you want to start a business and it's unconventional others may try to stop you to in order to prevent some disappointment—maybe that they don't want you to risk failure. They may ask "Who are you to start your own venture?" Think about it though: is that so risky? I argue that having a regular job is as risky nowadays as starting a business.

Now I want to take you back to some past times before we were alive. Before the Industrial Age took over in 1850s 80% of the people owned their business. So this isn't new. How did this work? What did people choose to do then? They found out what they were good at: crafting, farming, sewing, cooking, writing—and they offered what they created. This was true for thousands of years until we got into the Industrial age in the last 170 years.

So history has more of business ownership and doing what you love and you are good at. Then people traded their life and their passion to receive a paycheck every two weeks. People have given up control of being able to plan for their future. It was more secure and stable. But only for a while. According to new statistics more than 60% of people don't feel secure at their jobs no matter how many years they've spent with the company.

So this is what I remind people when they say it's too risky to do what they love or what they're good at; people used to do this for centuries until this system of hierarchy came about. Handing control of your life over to someone else's hand is relatively new. Unfortunately the education system prepares you for this type of work rather than being on your own and creating your craft whatever it might be.

I think the Industrial Age had taken a toll on people and unfortunately big companies are still run with the same principles; the new generation will not tolerate this type of control and will look for more meaning in life. They will make the changes happen sooner or later.

So no matter where you are in your life at least take the time to think about what your strengths are, what you love to do and turn it into a hobby. Who knows? You might turn it into something lucrative so you can quit the job that sucks all your energy. How nice it would be if we all created something we love? And if we understood we need to support each other to make a living doing what we love.

*"One day you'll wake up
and there won't be any more
time to do the things you've
always wanted. Do it now."*

— PAUL COELHO

# Your Legacy

What do you want your legacy to be? Have you ever thought about it as you go through your busy life? Why are we living anyway? Do you hope we can leave this place having touched one person or made a difference for something we care about?

What would you want people to say about you when you're 80 or 90 sitting on your porch? This is an important question to think about. Since our lives will come to an end, we want to feel good about what we did here before we leave. That's why I like living backwards. Where do I want to be before I die to make sure I live my life accordingly right now to the best of my ability?

Those small things you worry about: will they matter when you look at your whole life at age 90? What matters to you the most? Do you make time for those things today? If you don't, stop making excuses and do them anyway. Set your priorities and try to create a life that's aligned with what you care about. I know you may say, "But we all need to make money and make ends meet." I know, believe me. I lived on a month-to-month basis not knowing where my next money was going to come from. But no matter where you are in your life right now you can take the time to know your priorities, what matters to you the most, and align your life (at least put some thought into achieving a balanced life) accordingly. We all know life can be difficult but we can put some effort into making our priorities happen so when the end is near we can take a deep breath and say we lived a life that mattered. We created the legacy we wanted and we didn't only react to life but became an active participant in creating it.

I chose consciously to be the person who helps others see their gifts, to discover their passion and potential to share with the world. To me that means being authentic and learning the skills to make our lives more fulfilling. I would like to see businesses work with these values too. Whatever I write or say or speak or coach is about this goal. My priority is my family and friends and I'll arrange my life so I have time for them. I'm not a victim of my circumstances. I create my life to the best of my ability.

*"Stop waiting for Friday, for summer, for someone to fall in love with you, for life. Happiness is achieved when you stop waiting for it and make the most of the moment you're in now."*

— ANONYMOUS

# Yes, you're special

I believe in the simple truth that we're all special in our own way. That's why we don't need to put anybody on a pedestal like they're out of this world. They may be geniuses, creative artists or great speakers but you also have the same brilliance in yourself—just in a different way.

I know people who I think are amazing and out of this world. But I also realize making these people better than me because of their title put me into a place where I stayed small, sometimes very small. I know this isn't right. No matter where those people are or have been they're still human beings. The difference between them and you might be the fact that they know their calling and they're ready to fail and take risks when you're not.

Just as we don't want to belittle anyone or make ourselves look superior, we don't want ourselves to be smaller than others either. We all meet people who act only out of their egos and want to look special and rare. But think about this: If they were glad with who they're and satisfied with themselves would they really have the need to show off like that? I don't think so. If you read about successful people, in their definition of success they're very humble. They still say they don't know it all and are ready to help others be successful as well. They want the same for others.

So don't put yourself or others on a pedestal. We're all special in our unique ways going through life doing something important and being happy.

I believe in the simple truth that we're all special without our titles or roles in this world. We all deserve everything great just because we inhabit this planet. This fact also relieves us from that never-ending feeling of "never good enough" no matter what we do and what we achieve.

*"The difference between what we do, and what we're capable of doing, would solve most of the world's problems."*

— MAHATMA GANDHI

# "Your Best Life" story

I'm alive. I'm naturally curious. I can do anything. All is possible. I'm full of dreams. I'm capable. I can be my true self. There are few expectations of me. I can tell the truth: "I don't like you today", "You are fat." Everything is acceptable. Then I get a little older and by the time I reach school age, I'm not so free anymore. I need to behave in certain ways. It's not always okay to tell the truth. Well, didn't you teach me to be honest? What happened? When am I supposed to lie and when do I tell the truth?

How do I keep my livelihood and my essence alive?

Why do I need to study these equations and solve them on paper in math class when I know I have calculators that will help do it in seconds? Because our education curriculum is probably not updated as often as needed and the only thing we know is to repeat what we did last year. How come I need to know what I want to do with my life at 16 or 17 to make sure I choose the right classes to take me to college? How come I need to be so many things all at once? Very successful academically, being the team captain, playing the guitar for eight years in a row making sure I also get an award, starting my own non-profit as a teenager. Can we really do it all and not be burned out? So is this what my society thinks is best for my future?

And so we lose even more of ourselves with all these expectations.

Wow! My mom works so hard and gets laid off for the third time! What am I supposed to do so it doesn't happen to me? Which field is the best to pursue so I can afford a simple house for a family and also pay my student loans? Would it be worth going to college if I can't find a job to even pay my bills? I don't think my passion for music or sports will pay for my life in the future. So I need to listen to others and see which profession is best for me. Here I go, losing another part of myself and forgetting about my passion or having little time to enjoy it since I need to work countless hours to finish college in a field I don't even like.

Then if I'm lucky I'll get a job that pays decent money with some benefits. Not so bad while I'm single. Much better than the allowance my parents gave me. I'm happy. I achieved my goal. I'm successful. I can now make plans to have a family, own a house.

It's getting harder to accept what my managers ask me to do. I have this great trusting relationship I created with my customers but they want me to sell more although I know they have no need. This doesn't align with my values. Am I supposed to sell something my customers don't need and risk the long term relationship? Risking all I've built over the years? This doesn't make sense to me. And am I not supposed to voice my opinion if I see the business we're in is changing? They don't want to make the investment so I need to shut up. Hmmm, how do I do that? It doesn't feel right; it's not about me; it's for the business. What? They just laid off someone who dedicated most of his life to this company. Hmmm, maybe I should be careful what I say. Maybe I shouldn't get so attached to this company. They don't see me as a person but as a number. How do I keep my excitement at this job while the company is against what I believe in? But I need the money so I should see it as "just a job" and don't question it so much. Most companies are like this anyway.

Ooops, you lost a big part of yourself again. You can't be yourself and live your values in this environment.

You suddenly find yourself in your 30s and can't believe how your life has gone by so fast. Everybody's getting older but you're not supposed to reach your 30s so fast. Is this any indication that you'll also get as old as people you see on the streets? As your parents? Wow! I think I need to pay attention to how I spend my time. I really think I need to do things I enjoy more. But work and family and the financial burden seem to get in the way. How do I dig myself out of this hole? I don't think my job is a good match for me. But I don't know what's best for me anymore either.

Remember, you started losing who you really are since you were five? You're completely disconnected from who you truly are by now.

# "Your Best Life" story

Who am I? Why am I in this world if I'm not immortal and time goes by so fast? What should I do with my life? What are the most important things for me? You're lucky if you started asking these questions to yourself in your 30s. It's a process that may take years especially if you never listened to your heart and your inner voice that whispered in your ear for so long. But the good news is that it's possible. You can recreate your life again no matter what your age is. Colonel Sanders, founder of KFC, made it happen at 65. Darwin's scientific work didn't get recognized until he was 50. You just need to spend time answering some important questions but the journey is as joyful as reaching the end. I love it. I loved it when I did it for myself. I love it when I join the journey with my clients.

All of a sudden, at least at some point, you start to feel joyful and excited about your life again. It may not be a big drastic change in one day but as you drizzle more of what you love and more of what you're passionate about into your daily life, you feel so much more like yourself. You start to connect to who you really are and the best part is you always have it in you; you just need to take time to rediscover it.

Come and enjoy *Your Best Life*!

*"Take the first step in faith. You don't have to see the whole staircase. Just take the first step."*

— MARTIN LUTHER KING JR.

# Vulnerability

I don't think you can follow your passion, especially if it's considered a little unconventional in your environment, without being vulnerable.

Vulnerable means being totally exposed when people see who you really are. It's putting that poem out there knowing you may be criticized; it's sharing your painting that doesn't look like Rembrandt's; it's speaking your truth during a company meeting not knowing what reaction you'll get. But speaking your truth is definitely one cornerstone of following your dream. Some of you will have some naysayers who will try to stop you. There will be some who'll harshly criticize you and won't agree with you—but you do it anyway. Because in the heart of your heart this is what you believe in and you're not ready to listen to anybody but your inner higher voice. You know what your heart wants and you'd rather be disappointed than listen to others. You know you'll regret it all your life if you don't do it right now.

I thought being vulnerable was being weak but as I saw more people who were able to share themselves and their sorrows, their sore points and how they felt without trying to look good and just be themselves, I realized I admired that more. I started seeing this as strength rather than a weakness. It takes courage to look bad or be okay with making mistakes and showing what you think is weak in you. I understood that this only makes us all human. The more we share our struggles or challenges, the more we give the right for people around us to do the same. When we share and talk not only about our brave moments but also our dark ones, we see the common humanity in us. It makes us more compassionate toward others and even toward ourselves.

Just like Brene Brown says in *Daring Greatly*, falling in love is being vulnerable and we've all been there. How can you not be vulnerable when you really love someone? You can't be together if you can't open your heart where it can hurt the most—but we all do it. We even do it again and again after being hurt so many times.

I love to listen to leaders, celebrities or managers who've achieved a lot in their lives but talk the truth about the difficulties in their lives. It makes us all real.

Look around you; everything you see besides nature all started with somebody's dream: that chair, that beautiful vase, that book, that amazing painting, that building across the street, that car—everything! If the creators were afraid to share those gifts with us we wouldn't have them in our lives. We wouldn't have that book or music that inspired us. We wouldn't have that dream car that makes us feel so great. We wouldn't have the chance to connect with the ones we love at the other end of the world. So believe in your dream and be vulnerable to share your gifts. What if Ataturk, Martin Luther King, Mozart or that local craft store owner that you love chose not to be vulnerable? What would we miss? What do the people around you and the world miss when you hide your own gifts?

*"Success consists of going from failure to failure without loss of enthusiasm."*

— WINSTON CHURCHILL

# Journey of our Dreams

I believe we were all born creative and powerful. We have unique gifts we bring to this world. Everything is possible when we're young. Just watch children. Everything is a wonder for them. Their dreams are always big. (I never heard any child wish for a boring cubicle job for 20 years). The unfortunate thing is that most of us lose this precious part of us as we grow up; that part that has faith in ourselves and the gifts we have to share. We subconsciously seek so much approval from our parents, family or society that we give up on who we can become. It becomes more important to fulfill the expectations of others and follow the norms. We realize more appreciation and love by following the path we're given by the people who love us. If we're one of the rare ones who believe in our dreams, our parents try to talk us out of them to protect us from future disappointments. (The good news is that this is happening less now with more conscious parents.) As a parent I understand why we do that at a deeper level. We wouldn't know what to do with ourselves if our children fell flat on their faces while they were taking risks on their own. We have no idea how to handle our feelings. As it turns out, it's really about us—not them.

What's important is that we don't lose those precious gifts and that special calling. We can pick up where we left off. They're just buried under a pile of limiting beliefs we accumulated throughout the years. The only way to regain access is to get reconnected with ourselves. That happens when we start to take some time off, creating some silent time inside the crazy, hectic life most of us live. These silent times make us hear our soul. As we practice more "being" instead of "doing", being more aware and mindful, we hear the real voice of our soul buried under the voice of our ego. (Our ego has a purpose too; it's there to keep us safe from danger, but we don't have to listen to everything it tells us to do.) We start to differentiate between the two voices. We feel hunches and hear whispers. Our intuition starts to kick in.

As we get more reconnected with ourselves, we start to feel lighter, more joyful and have that sense of wonder we had as kids. As we practice doing more of what moves and inspires us, we start to feel happier and more fulfilled. Something feels "right". When we do what we love, we don't notice time flying by. We start to ask important questions:

"Can I get rid of this job that doesn't satisfy me?"

"Can I carve some time in my schedule to practice what I love?"

# Journey of our dreams

"Can I bring more meaning into my life?"

For some of us, this is all we need. We get connected to what we love and find a way to integrate that in our lives in the form of a hobby, new career or new business. For some, the next big hurdle is to overcome the resistance that shows up. Yes, although we're so excited finally to see our calling clearly, we may not embed it in our life right away. Crazy as it may sound, resistance usually comes up as we're called to do something big. We may also be paralyzed by fear—fear of failure or fear of success.

Now it's time to overcome these obstacles. First, we need to accept resistance as normal and do what we're called to do anyway. Fear of failure is real. We don't want to disappoint anyone. We've followed the path and made people we cared about proud (hopefully) so far. How can we switch to do something we love now? What will they say? What if we fail and lose what we already have? Again, the only way to overcome this is to face the fear and do it anyway. Read about people you admire. See how they took risks and failed many times but were persistent in following their dreams. We seem to see only the shiny, successful part of their lives. It's not like they didn't have self-doubt or fear; they achieved success despite those feelings.

Fear of success is a little harder to deal with. Most of us aren't even aware of this. We believe success only brings glory and joy, and that we're ready to embrace it all.

However, it isn't so easy to take all of that it in since we've been at a totally different energy level for a long time. Even when we declare it's not where we want to be, it's our comfort zone. We know exactly how this feels. We don't know how it feels to be vibrant and full of great energy on our own path. Although it sounds great on paper to achieve what we dream, it may not be as comfortable in an energetic or feeling level as we want it to be. We need to be open to feeling different and have faith that things will work out when we're in our own flow.

This whole process of realizing our dreams may look long and cumbersome, but many people do it—so can you. What's the alternative? Having a life we don't love? What will you think when you know you're close to the end of your life and you didn't even try? What do you want your legacy to be when you die? It doesn't need to make the headlines, but it has to be something that's meaningful to you and a reflection of who you really are. Think about Mother Teresa, Thomas Edison, William Shakespeare, Picasso or anybody else you admire. What if they were too afraid to act on their callings? It would be a different world. Think of all the objects around you. They all started as somebody's dream as well. What if they never created the things we use every day to make our lives better?

I support you in being ready to follow your dream and make this short life as meaningful as possible. If you think you'll fail every time you try, hire someone to keep you on track. You may need someone who makes sure you stay out of your way in becoming who you're meant to be to make this world a better place. Imagine if everybody was able to be their authentic self and live to their full potential!

*This article got published in the book Transform Your Life 2 in November 2014.*

*"Do you want to live a life out of circumstances or do you want to live a life out of great vision?"*

— Marianne Williamson in an interview with Oprah

# HELPING OTHERS TO REACH THEIR POTENTIAL

I always believe in sharing what helped me in my life and also helping others who are less fortunate than me. I feel it's my obligation to do this when I know more or have more than they do. And our lives get to be more meaningful when we care and do something for others.

When I think of all the children born with the same potential but not having the same opportunities, it makes me wonder how all children would grow up if they had the same social-economic circumstances. We know there are millions of children who can't get the nutrition or the education to be who they were meant to be. As soon as you give a child a chance to get healthy and get educated, their life changes forever.

So as I talk about the potential we all have, I especially care about helping children in disadvantaged conditions to believe in themselves and to have an education to change their future. Every child deserves this and there are many who don't have the means to do it. All children matter and they're all equally important. The closest to my heart are the children back in Turkey, my homeland. That's where I want to give back—to my own country where I was raised. I've been blessed to find out about an organization called Bridge to Turkiye where its founders had the same vision to give back to our home country and make a difference in children's lives. If you can even educate one child and make sure their basic needs are met, you've already made a difference. When we want to do something meaningful in our lives we sometimes think of large projects and big donations. I learned you don't need to wait until you can do that. You can start small and still make a huge difference. When a child knows somebody they don't even know cares about his/her life; that alone makes a difference. They know somebody believes in them. Once they're given the opportunity then they can see their own potential and have the courage to dream. I think this is huge. If the more fortunate ones can help those who don't have the same opportunities, our lives get better. When you get outside of your own worries and think about others, it enriches your life. You realize your life is so much better than others and you become grateful for what you have.

If you want to donate for a child to reach their potential to share their gifts with this world, you can go to www.bridgetoturkiye.org/donate. Imagine this: just because you give them hope or help them get an education, they might be saving other lives as doctors, teachers, engineers and more.

*"If today was the last day of my lie, would I want to do what I am about to do today? Whenever the answer has been "No" for too many days in a row, I know I need to change something."*

— Steve Jobs

# All the other Life Skills that helped me live a better life

*"Stop attaching so much
weight to being right.
In the grand scheme of things,
being right is insignificant
compared with being happy."*

— DEEPAK CHOPRA

# BEING HAPPY OR BEING RIGHT

It's amazing how much we care about being right. We have the tendency to go into a big fight about how to load the dishwasher, how a certain word is pronounced or where to park because we want to be right. We're ready to argue for hours or days even to prove we're right. When they don't listen and what we warned them actually comes true, we die if we can't say, "I told you so." "I" *with a lot of emphasis on it.*

We don't even listen when we're in a conversation because we're thinking about what to say next to prove our point.

Most of us know this is our ego. Our ego wants to feel superior and big. It's a big blow to our ego if we admit we're wrong or if we're okay with someone else winning the game.

I watched on a TV show one day where the host asked the couple who were arguing about the smallest things: "Do you want to be right or do you want to be happy?" This question stayed with me. Most of us who are going into these arguments, do it automatically. It's our way of being. It's human nature. However, we don't think about the cost of "always being right". We lose the connection; you can't be connected when you don't listen and only try to prove your point. There's no way the person you're talking to is getting anything out of this conversation or feeling heard or connected.

We lose the chance to be happy because we're spending a good amount of energy on being right. We lose the chance to really "be" with someone, the opportunity to see a new perspective, to be joyful and loving.

Next time you observe yourself being righteous, stop and don't say anything, but listen. Choose to be happy instead. (I admit it's hard but it opens up a whole new world for you.) That will be a great gift for all the people around you. Chances are they may give up being right too!

*"Be kind for everyone you meet is fighting a battle you know nothing about."*

— WENDY MASS

## Being Human

What I realize more and more every day is that we all have some level of pain and this is part of being human. When you learn more about human beings—how we function, how we all have our own wounds from the past—it's impossible to judge anyone. We're usually quick to comment on other people's behavior but we all have reasons to act in certain ways. We have our little stories that we made up about ourselves in our minds when we were kids. We have our ego that we have to protect for survival. We have those parts of us that we don't want anybody to notice. We build strong parts in us around our weaknesses and protect ourselves from getting hurt. When you look at someone and don't approve of or like their behavior, all you can say is that they're in their own pain body and this is how they learned to deal with it. We really can't judge anyone because we can never be in their shoes and understand exactly what they had to go through to arrive at this point. Yet we all strive for the same things: to be loved and to be understood. We're very simple yet very complicated. We're simple because we go through different experiences in life and that makes us more human; it's complicated because it's hard to understand and explain why we act in a certain way. We've had hundreds of small or big experiences that happen to us that have shaped who we are today.

The key for me is to see clearly that we're all pretty much the same. It almost makes me weep every time I feel this in my heart. We're so connected and we're much more alike than we think. We sometimes think we're the only one suffering or in pain and that nobody can understand us or that something is wrong with us to feel a certain way. This just isn't true. We're all human and part of being human is to have pain and feel suffering. When you accept that, it gets a little easier. Not that it reduces your pain, but you know this is part of life and there's no use denying it. For the most part we're not comfortable with feelings like pain and sadness. But it's okay to feel it and stay with it. The illusion that only good things will happen to us isn't a safe place to be. Our world is shattered with the smallest misfortunes when we have this expectation in life. We appreciate the better days when we know how it feels to be in pain. Life is a roller coaster, as one of my son's coaches said when he was eight. It's so true.

The most important thing to remember is that we're never alone feeling pain or suffering and it just makes us more human! I love you even with all your pain.

*"Whatever you do don't play it safe.
Don't try to fit into the system.
If you do what's expected of you,
you'll never accomplish more."*

— HOWARD SCHULTZ

# BEING OK WITH "NO"

**W**e were usually so hurt as children getting the answer "no" from our parents that we carry that over to our adult years. It seems stupid but a lot of us do it. Because we interpreted every no we got in our childhood as a rejection and not being loved enough; we're terrified to hear that word ever again. Do we still hear it? Of course we do but sometimes we avoid it at a very high cost.

We give up on our dreams, we give up on getting support, we give up on ourselves—just not to hear the word no. We take it personally. If we're selling a product and somebody says no we feel like they're rejecting us. It's the product not you! It's so hard to overcome this, it's almost necessary to get as many no's as possible so it doesn't have the same effect on you.

You need to remind yourself each time that it's not about you before you ask any question or extend any invitation to others where you might risk getting a no! When you ask someone to be part of an event, if they're interested in a product or extend a dinner invitation you're just sharing an opportunity and they have the choice to say Yes or No. Equally so. We all do. Don't we want to be able to say what we feel when we're asked? So why take it so personally and get heartbroken and even decide never to ask again? No is as valid an answer as Yes. We have to remember it's not about us; we're making up the story, believing in it and making ourselves miserable. Good salespeople learn this quickly; otherwise how can they keep asking others to buy their services and products if they take every no as a personal rejection?

Go follow your dream, build your company, complete your project, plan that event; do the fundraising close to your heart, have your services ready and be bold enough to ask everyone if they want it or support it. See it like extending an opportunity to them. It's not asking a favor. They always have the right to say Yes or the scary word No and both are okay! I think about Howard Schultz, the founder of Starbucks. When he was trying to raise money for his idea, he had 217 people say no out of 242 he asked. (Check out his book *Pour Your Heart into It*.) What if he was terrified of the answer "No" and gave up on his idea? How many of us would have given up even on the second or third no? This is one of the factors that make successful people different. They believe in their dreams and ideas, they show a lot of persistence and they don't take "no" personally. Let's consciously remember and accept that every time we extend an invitation to someone, we have an equal chance of getting yes or no. If we only live for "yes", we'll live small.

*"Be grateful for every second of every day that you get to spend with the people you love. Life is so precious."*

— MANDY HALE

## BEING THANKFUL FOR BEING HUMAN, WITH ALL THE UPS AND DOWNS

As I get older I realize how we're all so alike. We have similar hopes, joys, fears, disappointments and sadness. Unfortunately many of us feel like we're alone, especially with our not-so-happy feelings, and this makes us feel isolated or weird. We feel like we're the only one suffering and that nobody will understand what we're going through. Actually what it all means is we're afraid to share our common humanity. All our ups and downs, our fears, anxiety and sadness make us only more human. We all want to have a decent life and be happy; at least have more happy moments than sad ones.

We're rarely the only one who is feeling a certain way. If we can accept them as part of being human we'll have less suffering. We'll also have more compassion for others since we'll know they're going through their own stuff as well. We try our best with what we know, what we've learned and what we've experienced so far. Empathy and acceptance of our ups and downs will nourish empathy for others. Once in a while we compare ourselves with others and their life seems so much better than ours. You never know though. We usually like to share the best parts of our lives not the ugly side, so we make an assumption that all is great in their lives. That's not true. No matter what, everybody has their own version of their good and bad days.

When I'm out and about in traffic or in a crowd somewhere, I sometimes stop and look around. I see people who have their own drama in life yet everybody is trying their best to live a good life and provide for those they love. We all want the same basic things: lots of love, being safe and to be understood or appreciated by at least one person in our lives. Thinking like this warms my heart and I send those people I'm watching my best wishes from the deepest part of my heart silently in those moments. We all suffer in our own way in this journey we call life. It's so worth going through though even after very tough times. When I see parents who've lost a child to cancer or a terrible accident and still feel the urge to live and fight to make others' lives better then I know life is worth living. We shouldn't forget that we're actually never alone and we're all connected in some level no matter what we feel. We can be thankful for being human, with all the ups and downs.

*"But you have to do what you dream of doing even while you're afraid."*

— ARIANNA HUFFINGTON

# CHILDREN OF OUR WORLD

I think about children often, thanks to the great Turkish visionary leader Ataturk who dedicated April 23 to them. It's known and celebrated as National Sovereignty and Children's Day. What a beautiful and meaningful gift to the children!

Why do we care so much about children, besides the fact that we give life to them and love them from the bottom of our hearts?

Because they're our future, our world's future and we want to offer them possibilities to have a good life and help them become happy, fulfilled adults.

I've always cared about learning more about human potential. I believe we all bring something unique to this world and if we were given the chance to tap into the energy in ourselves, we would certainly have a different kind of world.

I've often thought about children who never realize their potential to become who they're meant to be; those who might have been great scientists, doctors, writers, engineers or artists who could make our planet a better place if they were given a chance.

I've taken responsibility to help children and adults realize their gifts and strengths so they can share them with others for the greater good of humankind. That also means knowing it's our birthright to be happy and deserve all good things in life. Happiness isn't reserved only for the lucky, the wealthy, a special class of people or a special race. If children grow up to value themselves and follow their paths, they become more fulfilled adults. If every child—no matter what their living condition is—has a good mentor or parent who tells him/her how special they are in their own unique way and that people are all the same, I think we would have more peace around the world.

I'm passionate about children realizing their potential. We hear stories about people with the most traumatic backgrounds who had unfortunate things happen to them becoming very successful. Did you read the book *Unbroken* or watch the movie? Laura Hillenbrand wrote the true story of Louis Zamperini. It's an amazing story of our human spirit and how we can stay unbroken no matter what we experience in life or how we start our lives. He wasn't considered to be the most fortunate or the smartest as a kid but he endured all kinds of torture and hardship during World War II and returned home to be an inspiration to others until he died at 97. His brother believed in him as a child and changed his life. When you look behind stories like this, the common theme is that they believed in themselves and their own inner power.

It starts with helping children have their basic needs met like food, clothing and shelter; from there it's important to believe in them. Even the smallest things matter. When I was a child I didn't know that a new pair of shoes could mean so much to children who are economically disadvantaged. But sometimes if all we do is *be* with children, listen well and help them believe in themselves, these might be priceless for a child.

I hope we can all touch a child's life so we can leave a better world than the one we found!

*"To be great, truly great, you have to be the kind of person who makes the others around you great."*

— MARK TWAIN

# CREATIVITY

I used to believe some people are creative while some aren't. I would only see creativity as a form of art. Then as I grew up I saw that there are many forms of creativity. Although the first thought is always a poem, a movie or a story there are many different ways to be creative. Coming up with a business idea, a new design for a chair, finding a different way to organize oneself, finding something playful when children are around, working in your garden, finding a gentler way to talk to someone you love—these are all forms of being creative.

I also found out that I find my own creativity in silence, when I can remove myself from the everyday chatter and listen to my soul. I need to relax and be myself to bring out my creativity. I realized that being creative is a reflection of who I am, the message I want to share with the world. It's something I would do no matter what. It's part of my life but it's not something where I expect a particular outcome. It's something that needs to be expressed no matter what.

I read about the creative brain in a recent book written by a Harvard professor. The author explains how the brain works and where our creativity originates in our brain. She tells how we're all creative from birth and it's not limited to only the Picassos or Beethovens or Shakespeares of the world. She also explains how it can only be accessed after meditation or any way of being in silence. She talks about scientific studies that have been conducted that proves this. Creativity usually stems from an inner silence, from listening to your essence, your intuition.

So take time to be yourself and find your creativity, no matter in what form or shape it shows up. You don't need to be a Rembrandt to call yourself creative. The tiniest opening of creativity can lead to full self-expression of you in the world.

*"Drop from head to your heart."*

— MARK NEPO

# Nature

Nature has a healing power over us because we're an extension of it. Why do we generally have similar feelings when we look at the beautiful mountains, the clear blue sky or the green scenery right before our eyes? It's almost like therapy to be in nature, to walk on the beach or in a beautiful forest, to watch the sunset or sunrise. I talk about practicing stillness, being in the now, meditation—and being in nature is definitely one form of practicing the stillness in the moment.

I had an article published in a book in 1987. I wrote about being in nature and how happy it makes me feel. I think I understood the peace nature gives me at a young age and I take every opportunity to feel being connected to Mother Earth.

I love to see the birds, the dolphins or the seals on my beach walks. I love to talk to them. I love to take my dog to the beach and see him so happy in the ocean playing with other dogs. They're truly aware of their connection too.

One of my happiest moments is seeing a bird building a nest near our garage door collecting my dog's hair to make it even softer on the little branches of its nest. I'm amazed how the birds weave baskets for their babies. Astonishing and very heart-warming to see the unwanted hair of my beloved dog being recycled this way. Those moments make me feel excited and happy. It's amazing to me!

Then to hear the little birds starting to sing in their nest and the mom protecting them from the crows. Or a plant that you've neglected and even threw away to the side yard starting to bloom. I haven't met anyone who doesn't feel amazed at what's happening in our backyards or parks or at the beach when these beautiful miracles happen.

We all react to nature and stay in awe with the miracles because we're also part of it. I wish we were as kind as the plants and animals are and didn't harm or kill any of the animals unless we're hungry. Nature, animals and plants are ahead of us in evolution. They know how to live without struggling, they know there's only now (if you have a pet at home you know exactly what I mean) and they only prey because they need to survive. It's never about power, about religion, about money or differences that they can't tolerate. I know how we feel when we're in nature will help humans to be kinder to our planet.

I loved this quote that came up on social media a while back: "There's no Wi-Fi in the forest. But I promise you'll find a better connection."

*"The difference between the impossible and the possible lies in a man's determination."*

— Tommy Lasorda

# Living in a Land of "Can"s

When I started living in the U.S., I started observing many things. I'm always ready to get out of the box so now I had the biggest opportunity to learn new things. How is this land different than where I came from? First of all, as it happens when we leave something behind, we see and remember all the great things. My home country's hospitality, our warmth, our history and what it brings with it is priceless. Whenever we go back, there's unbelievable love that surrounds us that our children only feel there. My son loves to go back to Turkey. He couldn't always articulate why at a young age but it was the love and care of our family and our rich culture and the liveliness of the city that captivated us each time we were there. And our wonderful Turkish cuisine. We love it. But when you're away, the longing for the good things we took granted is another kind of experience. Our wonderful beautiful city Istanbul, having tea facing Bosphorus, being in traffic at midnight (which isn't fun when you live there), the concert at a 100-year-old church, strolling in the streets with lots of people, staying out until the crack of dawn and eating "kofte durum" in the cold, meeting a few friends to stroll in the most ancient streets—are all priceless moments for sure.

When I try to observe what's different though, I think one important thing is the mindset in United States. It's a land of "we can, you can and everybody can". You don't get to hear people saying "I can't", "You can't". It seems like any dream is possible here. Like the energy and the vibe create more possibilities. I think this must be a result of founding a new country with immigrants who showed the courage to start something new, who were willing to start from scratch and leave all that was familiar behind. This type of personality is a dreamer and a believer. When you have millions of them you create a culture of possibilities. At least this is what I think is the reason for this "anything is possible" mentality.

You may like the city or not but one of the best examples of this is Las Vegas. Some big visionary looked at the desert and believed in creating a city that would be alive 24/7. They have hundreds of hotels where there are pools and waterfalls everywhere—in the middle of a desert. There's no shortage of anything. About 39+ million people visit Las Vegas every year and bring a lot of money for the economy. (The Culture and Tourism Ministry of Turkey said 34+ million people visited Turkey in 2013.) So more people visit one city than a whole beautiful country. Just because some people believed in this dream! If I had been the one to think of that idea in a desert area of my country a few decades back, there would be thousands of people who would have said I'm crazy and I'm almost sure they would have convinced me not to start the project at all.

When it doesn't snow they don't close down a ski resort saying they made a huge mistake; they find a way to make snow. When Walt Disney wants to create a place for families to have fun, he starts with a mouse character to build the huge enterprise Walt Disney Company. Only the two main parks in the U.S. have around 34 million visitors every year. What kind of dreaming starts with a cartoon character and gets this big?

I think this believing, thinking big and the "everything is possible" attitude makes this country different than many others.

*"Yesterday I was clever, so I wanted to change the world. Today I'm wise, so I'm changing myself."*

— RUMI

# Resilience

One thing that always amazes me since I moved to the U.S. is the resilience of people under worst conditions and suffering. I watched 9/11, I watched people with burning houses, I watched people who lost their young children at a shooting or their young daughter at a terrible murder case or their loved ones in a horrific accident. I couldn't believe how they stopped being angry and asking why this happened to them. They used these mountains and layers of feelings for the good of others. This is unbelievable to me. I'm in awe of people like this and I'm deeply inspired. I'm moved by their courage, their resilience, their strength and their choice to do something good. This must be the best form of being human—when you choose love and forgiveness over hate and fear and choose to be so selfless to protect others and fight for others' lives to be better than yours.

I personally went to a young girl named Chelsea's memorial at her high school years ago when she was raped and murdered; all she had wanted to do was run at her neighborhood park. I'll never ever forget her parents' and little brother's posture and strength as they shared their deep sorrow with many people they didn't even know. They moved mountains and passed legislations so the same horrific thing doesn't happen to other children. I have tremendous respect for them. And I'll never forget the wife who lost her husband at 9/11 when she was expecting their first baby and she was still so courageous and resilient.

I've learned people grieve in their own way and that it's possible to turn something unimaginable and horrific into something good. What an inspiration these people are.

I take my hat off to these people and I wish them all the love in the world for being the best examples of being human. I pray we all get to see the light even in the darkest times like they do.

*"Surround yourself with people who make you hungry for life, touch your heart, and nourish your soul."*

— ANONYMOUS

# Having control- really?

I sometimes can't believe how naive I was when I was in my teens and 20s. I had a good start to life for sure, luckier than most of the population in this world. Great parents and family, good education, great husband I met in college, marriage and expecting my first child. Pretty much fits the plan. I remember conversations with my friends. We mostly believed we could control our lives. I really thought I was in full control and if something fell out of plan, it was my mistake or failure. All had to be a smooth ride.

I still have a decent life, thank God but I've seen so many different things and had ups and downs in my life that taught me I'm really not in so much control all the time. You can have a plan, great intentions and the passion but there comes a time when you can't dictate what's going to happen next. My friends and I had shared some stories about experiences we wouldn't have imagined when we were in our teens or 20s. Why did I think we were so special? Why didn't anyone tell me life is full of surprises and that we need to expect the good *and* the bad? When I heard the basketball coach at my son's summer camp telling the bunch of eight-year-olds that life is a roller coaster I was shocked. In our society we don't say those things to our children. Maybe it's our over-protective child raising habits in my culture. I feel telling the real truth is better so there's not a huge disappointment when life throws you out of place. When life works well for me I say, "Sure I deserve it. I'm a good person." What about the young lives that are lost all around the world? What about a parent who loses their child to cancer? What about homeless, hungry children? Are they bad? Don't they deserve the best? Of course they do. Everybody is born with the same human rights but not everybody is lucky to get what they desire. So where is this entitlement for the best coming from?

Now I know better that anything can happen anytime. You really can't control your life 100%. There has to be some level of surrender and faith. That doesn't mean not making plans, or giving up on goals and dreams—but what I'm learning is to do your best and then leave the rest to Universe. If it doesn't happen it's not the end of the world and it's not *your* failure. Sometimes you do your best and things still don't work out (at least it seems that way or it doesn't happen in your own timing).

It's so crucial to believe in the big picture. Sometimes we go through rough patches; we resist; we don't under-stand it; we don't like it. But as Steve Jobs said you can only connect the dots looking backward. All those experiences teach you something to get you somewhere. If you have the faith, things do work out better. If you want to force the outcome and try to be in control of everything, it somehow doesn't work so well. Build your dream, think about the steps, plan for it and start executing them without getting attached to what the results may look like. You probably have a smaller dream than what the Universe can give you, so let go. Believe in yourself and your dream. Don't listen to the little voice (ego) that wants to be in charge of every-thing. I remind myself of this every day.

*"As you get older you'll understand more and more that it's not about what you look like or what you own, it's all about the person you've become."*

— ANONYMOUS

# MONEY

As soon as we read that word "money", we have different emotions that come up even before we notice it. It's one of the most delicate subjects to talk about. We all grow up in unique circumstances that gave us different meanings about it. It's sometimes called the "necessary evil". Why evil? We don't question why it's evil. Once we define money as evil we've already created a certain kind of energy around our money.

Most of us are raised with the notion of too much money being bad for us. If we believe this, there's no way to attract money. If we don't have enough of it we feel ashamed, we complain. And if we do make a lot of money we start to build guilt around it and we lose it. We've seen celebrities with millions of dollars who went bankrupt. Somehow money starts to run our lives instead of serving us.

When we see business people who charge an amount we're not comfortable with we judge them. Since we judge them harshly (even though we would love to have the confidence to ask the same amount for our services or make the same amount from our jobs) even if we have a good opportunity, we're too afraid to make the same kind of money as we know we'll be the one to be judged this time.

I didn't know I had limiting beliefs about money until I came to the U.S. I was watching Oprah, reading about Bill Gates and I admired how much money they could give to others to transform their lives—people who are total strangers in other parts of the world. That made me think how having a lot of money can serve others and make their world better. You can do more good with more money. Too much money doesn't mean it's evil and doesn't mean you don't deserve it. But as the wealthy tell us, if you can't give a dime of your dollar, you won't give away $1M of your $10M either. Most of the wealthiest people believe you have to help others in order to receive. Money shouldn't be all about you. Giving and receiving is the cycle that works.

I faced my emotions related to money when I started my own business. I had no idea how difficult it was to ask for money for my own services even though I believed in the value I was providing. It was so much easier to ask for millions from customers while I worked for IBM or when I did a fundraiser for a cause I believed in; but not so easy when I had my own experience and skills to share with people who wanted to receive them. I had to dig in deeper to understand my beliefs around money and the stories I created so I could let them go.

We all pay for things that we value. Sometimes it's a price that's expected but sometimes it's way above our budget because we believe what we buy is going to make us happier, healthier or wealthier in some way.

So if you see yourself judging others about their abundance of money see if you can find your own stories about money. How does it make you feel? Are your beliefs true? Catch yourself when you judge people with a lot or very little money. Does the amount of money you have in the bank define who you are? Do you attach money to achievement or success or feeling superior? How do you use your money?

Just pay closer attention; you may find some beliefs you can change that may take some weight off your shoulders. If you believe you deserve money, you may get more than you ever imagined and you can use it for a great cause you believe in. It's good to have a healthy relationship with money so it doesn't define you.

*"A man sees in the world what he carries in his heart."*

— GOETHE

# Ideals and Standards

Every time we start a sentence with "I should" it's better to check if it's accurate or not. Where does that come from? Who's setting our ideals and standards?

I have so many of them, I can't even list them here but when I stick to them all, I'm totally overwhelmed. I should work out at least three times a week. I should spend more quality time with my son. I should make more money. I should be available for all my friends when they need me. I should be able to take good care of my flowers. I should make healthier meals. I should get eight hours of sleep. I should keep the house clean. I should take my dog for a walk at least an hour a day. And the list goes on and on and on. I'm sure you also have a similar list.

There are also the other shoulds and shouldn'ts: I should never fail; I shouldn't suffer; I shouldn't feel this bad; I shouldn't waste my time worrying etc. Who said these? Where did we come up with all of this? Who said, "We should" instead of "I want to"? What if we changed all those sentences and replace "I should" with "I want to..."? That may give us a break. At least it will be something we choose rather than something we feel we "must". The energy of those words makes a difference. I've done enough torture to myself saying I should; that's why I know this so well. Do you know how it feels when you only made two of the 20 shoulds you had in one day? It's a big pressure. It's a perfect way to set yourself up for failure. Start the day with a long unrealistic list of things to do with the intention of completing them all and when you see what you did at the end of the way; you can feel like a total disaster. If you do this on a consistent base, it only gets worse.

I'm still practicing having a shorter, more reasonable list and working to drop "should" from my vocabulary. If I'm done with the three things I want and I choose (versus I should) then I can always add a few more and only if I want to. We all have busy lives. Have you heard anyone complaining how much ample time they have? I haven't. So we need to learn how to be kinder to ourselves.

I know not everybody is crazy like me. My husband is always busy yet fits a lot into his schedule and he's never overwhelmed like me. He isn't torturing himself like I do if he can't stick to his plan. He has his own shoulds but not like me. I go crazy. I feel bad. I feel guilty. I feel like I failed.

The ideals and standards usually start at an early age where we're trying to prove ourselves. They're usually what we heard growing up that we need to measure up "to be somebody". But I know better now; it's not what you do but who you are that makes the difference. You may succeed and you may fail but it doesn't change the essence of you who you are. You may not do your shoulds for months and it won't make you any less of a person.

Be kind to yourself and just make sure you know who you really are; remind that to yourself when all your list items don't have a check mark next to them. Watch your language and see if all your shoulds and musts are realistic or not and if not, change them to "I want to..." or "I choose to..." The vibration of these are a lot different than "I SHOULD" and "I MUST". You'll lift a pressure off your shoulders.

*"People rarely succeed unless they have fun in what they're doing."*

— DALE CARNEGIE

# Self-Expression

It's time for self-expression. Self-expression is an extremely important skill to learn or relearn. Why do I say "relearn"? Because as children we had this skill already. Yet some of us lose it when we're not given the freedom to express our feelings at a young age. We shouldn't be angry, we shouldn't say this or that because it's not nice. Then we decide with our young mind that there's something wrong with us and decide to shut down. We may have parents who are authoritarian and we feel fearful of expressing our opinions. Then these figures appear in the workplace or in partners and we continue to be quiet even when we have a strong opinion.

When there's tyranny or authority used for negative reasons there's no room for self-expression. The same thing applies in our families, at our jobs, at the nationwide level. Do you want to be followed and obeyed because of fear or because of respect? Which one lasts more?

If we realize the importance of being unique and truly ourselves, then we can start to relearn how to express ourselves. One way to achieve this is by making sure we don't make ourselves or others look or feel superior, even with our children. Just because we brought them into life and we have the age difference doesn't give us the right to feel like an authority. They have the same right we do to express themselves and their thoughts and opinions even if we don't agree. We want to guide them and tell them about life experiences we've had but it doesn't mean they have to operate in the same way we did. The best we can do is to set an example to be self-expressed in a constructive and kind way. The same applies in the workplace. The fact that you're a CEO doesn't give you the right to act or make demands like you're superior to your employees. You may have great skills that some don't have but there are others in the same organization that possesses other great talents you may lack. So this allows us to bring a different type of leadership in all areas of life.

This is what we need to ask yourself: Do you want your children to be carbon copies of you? Do you want people to respect you or be fearful of you? Do you want them to naturally follow you or just obey even if they don't agree? Who do you want to follow? What are the qualities that make you follow others with your own will? What's the impact of lack of self-expression? What do you lose?

I support you in striving to be self-expressed and willing to actively listen to others who are willing to share their feelings, thoughts and opinions with an open mind.

*"Be the change you want
to see in the world."*

— MAHATMA GANDHI

# It Shouldn't Have Happened to You

The other day I was watching an interview and one thing stayed with me. The two people were talking about life not going according to plan and how we respond to the "unexpected" as humans. The phrase we use mostly is what the person being interviewed said: "This shouldn't have happened *to me*". "To me" is the part that's emphasized here. I had my share of saying this I'm sure. The interviewer then asked the best question that should follow that common statement: "Who should it have happened to?" This made me laugh. So is it okay if it happens to "others" like a friend or relative, the guy across the street, somebody I never heard of in the newspaper? But it's not okay if it happens to me? And what makes us so special to be protected from all bad things? I think I never thought about it like this. It's so true though. When something bad and unexpected happens we question this fact but almost never when something good happens to us. So we deserve all the best and "others" deserve all the bad?

It's understandable that we don't want sad and bad things to happen to us or anybody we love. As moms don't we always pray especially for our kids' safety and well-being? Of course we do. This is part of being human but this statement made me think that as a member of this species anything that happens to "others" can happen to me as well—because in fact there are no "others". It's only "us" on this planet. We're all part of the whole. Accepting this doesn't mean we'll welcome misfortune and be happy about it but it makes us realize we're as ordinary as everybody else is. It's also a humble reminder to appreciate what we have NOW. We're not guaranteed any safety in this world from what we call bad or sad or misfortune. It can strike us all and we need to face it.

This made me think of being grateful for my life right now and that I'm not any more special than anybody else. Our lives can change direction in any minute of any day. So we want to be the best version of who we are and give it all instead of staying small. It also teaches us to practice living without *the need to know* what tomorrow will bring. Because no matter what we do, we really don't know the answer to that question. It's best to have faith that things will work out if you follow your purpose and stay in your own path without betraying yourself.

Let's be grateful for this moment now.

*"It's health that's real wealth and not pieces of gold and silver."*

— MAHATMA GANDHI

# BEING HEALTHY

I can't omit living a healthy lifestyle when I talk about living a better life. It's been proven over and over by scientists that working out and eating healthy makes us happier and live a better life.

My husband and I started our marriage with healthy eating habits right from the start. We exercised one way or another. But when we came to California where people really care about healthy lifestyle habits, I got to learn a lot more. Most of us have access to this information. Some of the facts about health change as new scientific studies are done but the fundamentals are the same. We need to be active which may be walking, biking, running, swimming or anything we enjoy at least a few times a week. Eating healthy which means eating lean protein and lots of veggies and fruit. We all have some weeks when we don't work out or those days when we eat delicious food that might not be as healthy as it could be. But if we keep it in balance we have a way to have a healthy lifestyle.

It's not always fun. Maybe we don't always want to be active. But if you remember your intention and the reasons for doing so you may find the energy to do it anyway. Make sure your activity is something you enjoy so it's sustainable—or change your routine and try different activities to make it more fun. Include friends or family so you motivate each other. Whatever works for you, JUST DO IT! Give yourself permission to eat what you love. Just eat smaller quantities if it has too much sugar, fat or starch in it. Or make sure you eat less after overindulging

This is my formula. When I was overweight I deprived myself of my lovely pasta plates and it didn't do me any good. As soon as my diet was over I was going to eat a pot full of pasta. When I understood I could eat whatever I liked but in smaller quantities and work out so I can burn some fat and gain muscle—the muscle we all start to lose in our 30s—my life got better and I dropped weight.

I feel a lot better overall when I'm active too. Working out isn't only for my physical well-being but also for my emotional well-being. That's how I start my exercise at the gym; I say my intention every time so my body and soul are already aligned working for the same goal. I suggest you find some activity you can integrate in your life even if it's only five or 10 minutes a day. It's always better to do something than nothing.

*"Knowledge isn't power until it's applied."*

— DALE CARNEGIE

# Knowledge alone isn't the only answer

We have more information at our hands than ever before. We're not lacking information when most of the news starts with discussions about "Big Data".

Data and knowledge doesn't necessarily make us powerful though. There are thousands of books about weight loss but many still can't do it. Do we have all the information? Yes we do. We all know how to lose weight but there are more and more overweight people every day. So knowledge alone isn't really enough.

Some of us have other business or personal goals we want to achieve and we mostly know how to get there. But we don't always apply what we know. Why? Because there are a lot of deeper feelings and barriers we don't often notice. When you have a wish like finding a great partner you may not be thinking of the fear of losing your freedom yet it might be there subconsciously blocking you from committing to someone you meet. If your fear is more powerful than your desire, you may not achieve your goal.

If you want to move somewhere else and you make plans but don't take action there's probably another feeling that keeps you there. I love the money exercise on this subject I've seen at seminars. When an audience is asked if they want more money all the hands go up. When you ask them to imagine how it will feel when they have all that money though, negative thoughts and feelings come up for some. They imagine a lot of people might ask them for money; they express a fear of being famous as a lottery winner, or the fear of losing it all, or feeling bad or guilty because they have so much. We usually don't see this part of the story often buried deep in our subconscious. We only know we want something. But there are conflicting emotions involved. These are usually hidden to us unless we put the work and time into going deeper.

Feeling your feelings fully, staying with them and understanding what lies beneath is a practice you can integrate in your life.

So knowing things with our logical mind isn't always the answer to reaching our goals. We need to understand our feelings attached to our desired outcomes. See if you can discover what's keeping you from reaching your goals and dreams even after you've accumulated all the required knowledge. If not and you still feel blocked, hire someone like a coach who can help you overcome the blocks.

"If there's one thing I've learned in life, it's to fight. Fight for what's right. Fight for what you believe in, what's important to you. But most importantly, fight for the one's you love, and never forget to tell them how much they mean to you while they're still alive."

— ANONYMOUS

# LOVE IS EVERYWHERE

Years ago I fell in love with the movie *Love Actually* written by Richard Curtis. If you haven't seen it I highly recommend it. The first scene starts with a narrative suggesting that love is everywhere although some may think there's too much hatred in this world. It suggests one of the best places to witness love is the arrival gate of an airport. You can watch people of all ages and nationalities hugging and kissing each other with love. It's a beautiful scene. If we pay attention we see a lot of love around us.

This is how I feel during holidays especially at times when I'm volunteering. Recently I was at the San Diego County Fairgrounds at a huge warehouse-like setting with hundreds of volunteers of all ages. The event was organized by a nonprofit organization for families in need. Thousands of items had been donated waiting to be organized for families to do their holiday shopping with their kids for free.

We had very easy tasks to do like sorting, organizing and counting. The beauty of it was the amount of donations gathered. Toys for the young ones, the coats to keep children warm, bicycles, food, small treats for the parents. It was so heart-warming to be there and see the love for people we didn't know; the caring and sharing that every-body wanted to be part of. The person in charge of our group was telling the stories as we walked around. They wanted to make sure no kid has to look down and say "no" when they were asked if they got any Christmas gifts when they go back to school. They told us some parents cry when they finally find the toy their kid has been longing for during those free holiday shopping days organized for them.

These types of events help me believe in our humanity and that there are millions of people who want to do good even when they're going through tough times themselves. It was hard to believe all those items were still not enough for all those in need but it's still wonderful to think how many people are going to be happy during the holidays—having food at their table and gifts their kids can enjoy.

I had the privilege of volunteering at many great events like this, doing something for people I didn't know. Those are some of the best moments of my life.

I leave those events feeling grateful for all I have in my life but mostly grateful that there are many giving warm wonderful hearts in this world. Look and you will find love everywhere.

*"Love yourself. Forgive yourself. Be true to yourself. How you treat yourself sets the standard for how others will treat you."*

— STEVE MARABOLI

## Loving ourselves

Years ago when one of my friends told me we should learn to love ourselves, my inner voice said, "I already love myself." I felt pretty content with my life and who I'd become.

You know some statements stick with you for a long time. This was one of them. What I realized over time was that I only loved the parts of me I find to be "good" or "strong" as I define it in my own world. I only loved the parts of me that were admired. I knew then that's really not the definition of loving yourself.

Loving yourself means being loving and kind to yourself even in the midst of those dark moments when you see your own weaknesses. It's not loving yourself if you're only happy with who you are when you're your bravest or in your most joyful and giving moments. It's easy when everything goes well. What most of us need to work on are the times when we realize we didn't live up to our own ideals and standards. In order to say, "I love myself" you need to accept who you are completely with all your strengths and weakness, successes and failures. (What do all these mean anyway? Who defined these words for you? Well that's a whole different subject on its own. But something to think about.)

The self-love I talk about here comes from the heart; it's gentle, spacious, forgiving and compassionate. It's not your ego that makes you more special than everyone and brings arrogance.

The secret isn't to judge yourself when you feel like you're "less" or you make a mistake or the life doesn't go according to plan. You need to be okay with yourself first and love those parts of you that don't make you proud. That doesn't mean you don't want to get better at some areas of your life and try to become a better version of who you are. You can still do that while loving yourself. We all make mistakes, we all "fail"; that's what makes us human. We don't need to show others that we're perfect because none of us are. If we accept those parts of us that we don't really admire as being part of being human and be open to get better and learn something new, there's no failing. That's when we can embrace ourselves and love us just the way we are. The miracle is that when you're less judgmental of yourself you treat others better too. You already know everybody is on their own journey with their life. It also makes you feel you're not alone and everybody has their own miracles and struggles. You become less judgmental.

I suggest you try this meditation. Close your eyes. For a minute imagine you're walking on the beach on a beautiful warm sunny day. And then you see a 4-year-old coming towards you, totally innocent and full of life. When she gets closer, you see that it's you at that age. Go hug that child and tell her how much you love her. That she deserves all the love in the world and there's nothing wrong with her. That's the kind of love we need. When we love ourselves with all the strengths, gifts and weaknesses we have, we're able to love others more. That's how love spreads around the world.

So go ahead and think about whether you *really* love yourself. See if you can feel it when you say the "wrong" thing at work, when you get angry at your child because you had a bad day, when you feel like you don't make the money you deserve. If you can't do it try this: Think about all the people around you who you support when they're having a difficult time in their lives. Do they still deserve love? So do you! Think about when you were an innocent child who broke things around the house and still deserved the care from your parents. You're still that child within you. It's okay to make mistakes and still deserve to be loved—even by you!

*"The privilege of a lifetime
is being who you're."*

— JOSEPH CAMPBELL

# WHAT DO YOU WANT OUT OF LIFE?

When we're asked the question, "What do you want out of life?" we often stop and wonder as it's not so easy to answer it right away. The first things that come to mind are usually "to be happy", "to be rich", "to be healthy" however in reality we're not so sure what we really want out of life. We think being wealthy will solve all our problems and we have such a demanding life that health doesn't even become a priority.

We seem to get busier juggling dozens of things on a daily basis that we lose our connection with our essence, our soul. We don't stop even for a minute to see what we *really* need and want deep inside. We're only *reacting* to life not *creating* our own. (If you do create your life, give yourself a big hug ☺. That's huge.)

Nobody says it's easy to discover what we *truly* want out of life but with some awareness and tools, it's not impossible either. I believe it's worth stopping and finding the answers before it's too late. We need to start noticing when we feel excited, when we want to have more of something, when we feel peaceful or joyful. Who are we with at that moment? What are we doing? What do we see? Where are we at our happiest moments? These are good clues. No matter how busy our schedule is, we can find time to integrate these powerful moments into our life. This time spent devoted to our deep thoughts and feelings let us see our light and our gifts. How come we're okay not sharing our talents and strengths with the world? Some people even create a whole new or career out of this journey; whatever the outcome is, this discovery helps us feed our soul. We'll have better answers for our purpose in life. We'll feel more fulfilled and peaceful.

Nobody is proud to have been busy or to have had an important title or a super clean house when they're about to die. Everybody wants to look back and remember those happy moments doing the things they loved and being with the ones they loved. It's so valuable to take the time to find out who you are and what makes you happy deep inside so you can create your own version of a great life: *Your Best Life!*

*"Don't look back, you're not going that way."*

— Anonymous

# PLACES HAVE THEIR OWN ENERGY

Do you ever feel more energized or more comfortable in some places than others? It might be a friend's house or a coffee shop or a town you're visiting. I believe something matches with our energy in those places. I've been lucky to travel and see new places and some I call beautiful but some make me feel inspired or more like myself. My trips to the U.S. always made me feel different when I was younger. Although this was a foreign and far away land, something always felt good as soon as I stepped foot on U.S. soil. Some coffee shops I love because they boost my creativity. Some towns I visited made me want to stay a lot longer than my vacation time there. I also have some friends' houses that make me feel very comfortable and happy when I visit. Some feel so cozy and lovely.

When I was reading Eckhart Tolle's book *The New Earth* I was excited to read how he moved to the U.S. based on his intuition and he wrote his books here. That made me feel so good. I've often wanted a good answer to give to people when they ask me why I moved to San Diego, California. It just felt right. I love the energy, the vibe here. Why was I not able to say it like that? I was always thinking of a logical answer to give. Tolle talks about different countries having their own energy. It's so true. The energy in my native country and the country I chose to live in have completely different energies. It's just a feeling you can tune into.

I think it's best for us to take the time and effort to be where we feel happy and comfortable. That could be a corner of your house or your yard; it could be a local park or the beach; it might be a little town you've visited or a country that you've been to because you feel more relaxed or alive there. Be present to that great feeling. Who knows what you'll create for yourself in those moments when you're there?

*"No amount of guilt can change the past and no amount of worrying can change the future."*

— UMAR IBN AN-KHATTAB

# PRAY MORE WORRY LESS

I bought this phone case I love that says "Pray More Worry Less". I wouldn't have picked this one up five years ago. My sweet grandmother taught me how to pray when I was younger. In the heart of all religions I still believe there's good for all humanity if we're able to practice it without making anybody else "wrong" or "bad" just because they don't share the same faith. I do believe in oneness and that we're all part of a big collection of creation—and something bigger than us that we call God or the Universe or Higher Power. If all religions were tolerant and accepting of each other then I'm up for it. I respect people who are religious as long as they don't kill others for the sake of their own faith.

In recent years, I got to know more about the universal laws, the power of prayer and how we get our questions answered when we pray. I learned the true meaning of "praying" out of a religious context. It's the expression of what you want and desire in life. It's a positive conversation with God or Universe or something more powerful than us. A close friend of my mine told me about her every-night ritual where she starts with meditation (which does make me calmer and more peaceful) and follows it by prayer. I've been doing the same ritual for the last four to five years. I also include my gratefulness prayers too. Praying (like in the book *Eat Pray Love* by Elizabeth Gilbert) gets me to a better place in my soul and gets me connected with Universe in a profound way to get my wishes realized. There's something magical about it.

Although I'm very positive in many ways, I also have worrying in my bones and it got worse since I became a mom. So my instant inclination is to worry about things that never happen! When I get present to it and know how much energy is wasted I look for ways to heal it. Especially when I hear the studies like "90% of things we worry about either happened in the past or will never happen" I want to make sure I learn how not to worry. When you pray you stay in the positive. You're praying for things to be better, you visualize what you want and you think about positive images when you pray. I love the phrase "worrying is a misuse of your imagination". So true. Let's reserve our imagination for positive images. Also by praying we let our vulnerabilities show. This makes us more humble and creates peacefulness in itself.

Praying has positive in it and worrying has negative in it. So that's why praying with the meaning (wishing things to get better and dreaming about what you want in life) is certainly better than worrying. I have the constant reminder on my phone!

*"Worry is a misuse of your imagination."*

— DAN ZADRA

# REGRETS OR DISAPPOINTMENTS

I feel like there's a big difference between regret and disappointment. I'd rather try things, take risks and fail rather than *regret* all the things I didn't do in my life. I've had my own share of disappointments in life and I'm sure there's going to be more, but I want to have the satisfaction of having at least tried.

As protective parents sometimes we'll do anything to prevent our children from feeling disappointed and we'll talk them out of some adventures they want to take or new things they want to try. This may be one of the worst things we can do to them. We may be killing their creativeness, their aliveness, their potential. I'm guilty of this too. It's difficult to watch your kid feel disappointed. But we just have to let them try and learn from experience; and the best part is despite our fears they may even succeed. Who would ever start a business if they wanted to prevent disappointment at all costs? The most successful entrepreneurs are the ones who failed, who felt disappointed over and over again but still had the courage to go on.

# Regrets or disappointments

Helen Keller, as you probably know, became deaf and blind when she was 18 months old but she never gave up on her life. She had to go through many disappointments until she graduated and wrote her book but she never had regrets of having not tried. There are so many stories about the athletes, the artists and everyone who had the courage to seek what they wanted to make a dream come true.

So let's not limit ourselves or our younger generations and let's have the courage to go after our dreams—and encourage others to do the same. We can let our children see it's okay when some of our plans don't work out; that we can use our persistence and belief to go on. When we're older, I think we all want to look back and say, "I did everything I could to live the life I wanted. Sure there were many disappointments and heartaches but I'm glad I always tried. Now I have no regrets!"

Disappointment can happen when you try no matter what, but with regret, you never even tried.

*"No one has ever made himself great by showing how small someone else is."*

— Irvin Himmel

## Self-compassion

When I was growing up, especially as a girl, thinking about yourself before others was considered being selfish. You always had to be polite, kind and respectful and it was the biggest virtue to think about others' needs before your own. This made me think I was a nice person. And if I ever thought about my needs and my wants first, I felt like a bad and selfish person.

As an adult, when I started to be more aware of what I say to myself in my mind, I realized I was beating myself up for the smallest things I couldn't do. If I don't walk my dog every day I'm a horrible dog owner. If I don't have a healthy dinner prepared for my son, I feel like a bad mom. If I'm not available for a friend in need, I'm a terrible friend. The list goes on and on. Then one day I read in a book that it's best to treat yourself as a close friend. Now when I catch myself saying horrible things to myself and feel guilty about something I didn't do, I imagine a girlfriend telling me the same story and sharing her feelings. I have so many nice things to tell her! I understand why she wouldn't always have the time to do the things she wants for her kids or her family or her friends. It's so normal. We're all human and we can't be perfect all the time. I would tell her, "We have good intentions darling. Sometimes we can't do everything we want. We have our good days and bad days. Why beat yourself up? Be nice and kind to yourself. It's okay. Please don't worry." These are things I would say, not only to calm her down and make her feel better but because I believe it's true. Life isn't that smooth and straight forward. So why isn't it true for me? Why do I have so much compassion for others but not for myself?

I know at least part of the answer. I was brought up to be the best in many things and I was taught to be selfless. I was raised to have compassion and empathy for others. These are all wonderful but I guess we could do better with ourselves too. I know some of us are great at this but many women aren't. If you're like me, listen to what you say to yourself when things don't go according to your plan and you don't accomplish 100% of your tasks. Think about a good friend who would tell you about her worries that are exactly what you feel now; I'm pretty sure you'll have some kind words to say to her. Make sure you turn that around and have thoughtful and compassionate remarks for yourself too. Say, "It's okay" and take a deep breath because you deserve it. Practice some self-compassion every day! You deserve it as much as your friends do.

*"Many of life's failures are people who didn't realize how close they were to success when they gave up."*

— THOMAS EDISON

# PERSISTENCE

When we look at people we consider to be successful we may think it was easy for them. They had the "right circumstances" or they had the brains to do it. So it's only for "them" not "us". We keep them at a distance from who we are when we think that way.

When you start reading about their biographies, you realize most of them faced many difficulties in their journey and failed many times—but they persisted. They didn't take it personally and let it stop them—they kept on trying. When you look at the qualities of people who achieved their dreams there's one common denominator. No person or no barrier stopped them from going forward in the direction of their choice. They believed in themselves and showed enormous persistence.

Here are some examples you may all know: Henry Ford's first five business ventures failed and left him broke five times before he founded Ford Motor Company one of the biggest car manufacturers of all times. Walt Disney went bankrupt after failing in several businesses. He was told he lacked imagination. Can you believe it? Albert Einstein was believed to be mentally handicapped. And the most well-known is Thomas Edison who made 10,000 attempts before he invented the light bulb. His teachers also believed he wasn't intelligent enough.

So when you think it was only their brilliance that brought them to their results don't underestimate the power of the persistence they had—enough to see their dreams realized.

"A meaningful life isn't being rich, being popular, being highly educated or being perfect...
It's about being real, being humble, being able to share ourselves and touch the lives of others.
It's only then that we could have a full happy and contented life."

— ANONYMOUS

# LEADERSHIP

I think we saw the best form of self- expression at Gezi Park, Istanbul at the end of May, 2013. Protecting one of the few parks left in the center of the city, young Turks started a peaceful protest. They showed the life they wanted; a life in peace, in unity, with compassion and love for one another. They created a small version of the world they wanted to belong to with their creativity, humor and all forms of art, sharing everything they had and helping each other when in need. They told everyone that they didn't care about politics or the parties, they simply cared about human rights. They refrained from being violent even when they were knocked down on the streets with water cannons, they couldn't breathe from the tear gas and they were injured. They warned each other to keep calm and quiet.

They showed us they cared about the environment, their responsibilities as citizens of the world and what it means to stand for something you believe in—with courage. They were true to themselves and their country. Everybody who was lucky enough to step into that park felt the humanity, the love and the happiness in the middle of all the chaos. Because of this, they were able to inspire millions.

This is what you want to see if you're a real "leader". Authentic leaders want to hear what others have to say even if they don't agree; they create an environment where others can be self-expressive and creative. They understand every individual is unique and how this collectively makes everybody stronger. True leaders give space to their people to be themselves. This is true in families, in businesses and in nations. If you're a parent, a manager or president of a country you want to inspire and move people; you want people to follow you because they respect you, not because they're scared of you. Think about authoritarian father figures; their children can't do anything but obey them. Or the CEO who insists he has the right answers to everything and isn't willing to hear new ideas. At some point the people they lead build up resentment against their leader. Scaring people with power and authority doesn't work in the long run in any context.

Think about all the leaders in your life: which ones did you like? The ones who gave you no space to be yourself, micromanaged you and asked for total obedience or those who were humble, who listened to what you had to say and inspired you? Are you a powerful leader in your life?

*"Life is about using the whole box of crayons."*

— RuPaul

# SELF-WORTH

Everything we do or don't do all comes down to our self- worth. Can we receive something with grace? Can we ask for something big knowing we deserve it? When we make decisions about our future is it because we really want it no matter what or is it to impress someone or get somebody's approval to be proud of us?

If we have enough self-worth, we do things for ourselves; if we don't it's usually to please others, get their approval or impress them. We do things to feel like "we made it" in the sense our environment defines it. It's great to feel the love and appreciation and to impress people but these needs are mostly in the ego satisfaction level. Where we want to be is to feel fulfilled for who we are, knowing it's our birthright to deserve and have what we want. We are worth it!

I think I achieved everything I knew I deserved and got stuck when I felt like only certain people deserved extraordinary things. I didn't know my dreams were limited to what I thought I deserved. Thinking BIG dreams was only for special people, not me. When I understood that everyone is special I saw that it's just our beliefs that hold us back from achieving bigger things in life. It's not our capabilities or strengths but how we think and what we believe that affects how we live our lives.

If you realize that EVERYbody deserves a good life despite their circumstances, their talents, their abilities and where they're born, then you know you can dream big and achieve those dreams.

I wish I could help every child understand that they deserve everything good! That would change a lot of things. Knowing your self-worth will set you free. It will allow you to feel great no matter what others say or think about you. You don't need anybody's approval to be worthy. You're already worthy of everything, just by being born!

"'I've learned that people will forget what you said, people will forget what you did, but people will never forget how you made them feel."

— Maya Angelou

# UNITY

I loved everything that unites people since I was a child, what brings people closer. Even the rain, because it brought my whole family under the same roof when we couldn't go outside on those summer days. Then I hate all things that divide us.

We all have our differences. We all come from different races, have different skin color, different likes and dislikes, different cultures and different beliefs. We support different teams. That's the beauty of being human. How boring it would be if we were all exactly the same and had the same passion for the same things. These differences make us unique and we should all celebrate them in ourselves and others. When these differences become a reason to separate and divide us however, then it harms the whole of humanity.

Nobody has a right to put themselves on a higher pedestal and think they're better, greater or more powerful because of their skin color, religion, age or the office they hold. This is true in families, in nations and in the world. What happens to us at this moment is a combination of many events and people we've met and we don't have control over them, so how can we judge and belittle others? Were you able to choose where you'd be born consciously? So why do you think you're better than any other because of your nationality or your skin color?

I grew up with Jewish, Armenian, Christian, Orthodox and I didn't know we were different. We didn't care. We wanted the same thing in life: to live a dignified life as human beings in peace.

It's tough to watch what's happening around in the world where there's so much division, so many bad leaders who encourage it even among their own people.

Unity is what we need in this world and we should stop bringing our differences out in a divisive way and cherish them instead. We all share this beautiful planet and we're here as visitors for a while. Let's share our common humanity and realize we're all one.

*"Be someone you want
to be around."*

— ANONYMOUS

# What's your excuse?

I loved watching the Olympics since I was a child. It makes me feel and think about many aspects of life and human beings. How these people found their calling at a young age, how incredible the human body is, the fame and pride that comes to medal receivers and how all the athletes inspire us.

I especially enjoy watching athletes who are disabled; it's such a big inspiration to me and others. When you see someone whose legs were amputated before she was a year old and see what she's available to accomplish in 34 years, my only question to myself is "What's your excuse?" I'm not asking this in terms of being an Olympian but for anything I want to accomplish in life. One of the disabled athletes I've admired is Amy Purdy. She has lived and breathed snowboarding for most of her life, but when she lost both of her legs as a teenager and her slope shredding days seemed over, she pushed herself to keep going. Having won the bronze medal at the 2014 Winter Paralympic Games in Sochi, Purdy is also an entrepreneur and launched a nonprofit to help other athletes like her.

# What's your excuse?

I don't tell this story to make everybody feel bad. We hear every day about people who go through rough times and understand the value of every extra minute they're given to live. There are athletes who accomplished a lot more after their journey with cancer. I don't want to be one of those people who looks back and regrets all the things they haven't done or at least tried. Not having time isn't an excuse when I look at mothers who raise six children and can still have time to work out. If I had the drive these athletes have, I could do anything. Believing in yourself, believing you're not different than anybody else, understanding your unique qualities and abilities can work in your favor, knowing that if you set your mind to it and work hard you can achieve anything. These are great virtues we can imitate.

Watching them makes me think again about all the great things I want to do that I'm putting off. I know that no other day than today is promised, so why not start now? What's my excuse not to race in my own lane of life and be the person I want to be? What's your excuse?

*"I'm stronger, smarter, happier and wiser...gee isn't this the truth. Learn from the past mistakes and move forward."*

— Anonymous

# Attitude

Our attitude is so much more important than what our circumstances are. I've watched so many people in my life and in documentaries who have the worst living conditions but they have a happier life than the wealthy people around me. If you watched the movie *Pursuit of Happyness*, based on Chris Gardner's nearly one-year struggle with homelessness, directed by Gabriele Muccino you know what I mean. He turns his life around from being homeless to having a multi-million dollar brokerage firm.

Science is looking into this more in depth. Some of it seems to be genetic; do we see the glass half full or half empty? Some of it is what we experienced as a child at home and from people around us. How did they react to different life events? We sometimes mimic them.

The key to our success has a lot to do with our attitude. Even how we interpret success comes from our attitude. If you say can or can't, you're right in both cases. The way you think and interpret what's happening around you or to you determines your experience. If you catch yourself before you react to a certain situation, you can change the course of your experience. If you're on autopilot and many of us are, then you keep living with the same habitual reactions and emotions. You can change your whole meaning and attitude about what's really happening—through awareness.

A typical example is when someone doesn't call us back and we make many meanings out of it. If we said something we weren't so happy about when we last met, we think she's upset with us. Or we think she doesn't care about us. We never think there might be something in their lives we're not aware of that might keep them from calling us back. We almost immediately jump to conclusions and believe them. It seems like we usually assume the worst.

I see people who receive bad news about their health but still have a good attitude about it that gives them energy to fight the disease and keep their chin up. They don't only affect their own well-being but also have a huge impact on people like me who watch them and are inspired by who they can be.

Having a good attitude or practicing to have a good one can change our lives. Check your attitude throughout the day, especially at difficult times. Know that you can choose the attitude that serves you and others best.

*"Comparison is the thief of joy."*

— THEODORE ROOSEVELT

## Juggling our Lives

We all want to have a balanced life. Especially if we start to really think about what life means and realize it goes by pretty fast. It's not so easy though. We know and do too much now.

When I got through my day, here are things I try to squeeze in. I want to start my morning with a prayer and good wishes to make it a great day. Then I want to have a healthy breakfast; for that I need to shop beforehand and make sure I have all ingredients available. I want to spend some time with my dog and walk him. I also need silent time to stay calm and stop my fast-paced thoughts for at least 10 minutes. I want to be at my desk at 8:00 am. I need discipline to work from home so I imagine I'm going to an office to make sure I get the most out of my day. Then I take a break (to continue being productive throughout the day). I want to be with my dog. He's too lonely without me. During lunchtime I want to get some exercise. I need to stay active to stay healthy mentally and physically. I don't want to extend my lunch hour too long to stay on track so I sit down at my desk. Ooops, I skipped lunch. That's not good. I go prepare a healthy lunch. If my son is at home

# Juggling our lives

I want to be there for him, to spend at least some quality time. Back to work. It's 5:30 pm. I know there's a lot more to do but I stop. Take a shower. Do grocery shopping so I have healthy food to eat.

Is there any time to relax? No! Let's get dinner started. I don't want to be in the kitchen until 9 pm. Dinner time is quality time with my family. Let's get together. I'm glad my son is home today. This is the time to connect and understand what's happening in his life. It's already 8:30 pm. I can't do the dishes now. I want sit down time. Watch TV a bit but there's nothing good on. Maybe I should read or write. I have friends texting me so I'll answer them. Oh wow it's 10 pm already. Let me go to bed and read a little. Don't forget my ritual: say my prayer, my gratitude and my wishes. Okay it's midnight already. Go to sleep to get seven to eight hours of sleep.

Next morning I get up. Shoot I forgot to do my leg stretches for my pain yesterday! I will make sure I do it today.

This is one typical day and I know you have a similar or even busier version of it. It's not easy to have a balanced life but knowing our priorities makes it a little bit easier. We can all establish our priorities each morning to have a more balanced day.

*"We are what we believe we are."*

— C. S. LEWIS

# WHAT YOU BELIEVE SHAPES YOUR LIFE!

It's crucial to sometimes stop and think about what you believe. If somebody makes wild guesses about your life or what you'll end up doing or how you'll look, before you take it as a fact you need to question it so it doesn't become your truth.

When you believe you'll be fat, you'll be fat. When you believe your life will be full of struggles, you'll have them. If you think there's a lack of money, you won't receive enough. Once you believe in something without questioning it, you create your life around it.

If you see yourself as someone who can't have a large impact, you'll stay small. You won't see the possibilities. When you think you have to live where you're born and can't leave, you'll never look at other options.

Sometimes life brings opportunities to review our beliefs and we see it doesn't have to be that way. We realize we have a say in our life and we can make a different decision. Be careful what you believe in. Question all your beliefs!

*"Have no fear of perfection.
You'll never reach it."*

— SALVADOR DALI

# Consider you're perfect

As I get older I know "perfectionism" isn't good for us. It's only to cover up what we think is wrong with us or it's a finish line that goes further away every time you try to reach a goal. It never ends; there's always better. Striving to do the best is different. You want to put all your great energy into accomplishing something without expecting that everything will go right. None of us are perfect.

In another context though, we're already perfect as we are. That means what we've achieved, what we've experienced and what we've brought to this world is already good enough. It's how it's supposed to be. We don't need to change anything about us; we only need to get rid of what gets in the way. If we knew we were perfect as we are in our essence, we wouldn't create all the suffering. Our goal should be to get back to our core self and get rid of all the learned judgments, expectations, ideals and standards we took on as we grew up. Just consider that all you had to experience, all the misfortune you faced, all the sadness you felt were to bring you closer to who you really are. These only forced you to feel certain things and understand certain facts of life and about yourself. If you don't listen or feel those emotions, life throws out even more of the same at you.

You know about those patterns; you know someone who attracts the same type of guys over and over. Or people who make money only to lose it again and again. Life is trying to teach us something and until we face it and see it, it keeps happening.

So just for a moment believe you're perfect and complete as you are. You're exactly where you're supposed to be.

Don't try to be a perfectionist to cover up something wrong or to impress; just embrace your perfect being.

"Create the highest, grandest
vision possible for your life, because
you become what you believe."

— OPRAH WINFREY

# Ignorance isn't bliss for me

I always want to know the truth even when it hurts. I want to know if something I do makes me an annoying mother. I want to know how much money I need for a comfortable retirement even if that number is scary and looks unachievable. I want to know if I'm healthy or not. I want to know if I do a good job at work or if I suck big time.

I think knowing the truth gives us a chance to do something about it. If the money I need for my retirement is too big of a number I have the choice to set that as a goal and work accordingly or downsize my life to reduce my expenses and change how my retirement life will look.

If I know I've got six months to live (God forbid) I want to make sure I only do things that matter to me and don't waste even one minute with daily worries.

I want to know what matters to me in life so I live or at least get closer to living doing those things.

I think being proactive and having a real goal makes life better. Otherwise we're working and keeping ourselves busy for no good reason and we're only being reactive to what happens. Then we feel weak and out of control and don't see that we're the creators of our life every single day. We wake up one day and don't even know why we work and why we do what we do every day. It's important to know what you want to do with your life and be conscious about it.

So I really don't think ignorance is bliss even when the truth seems unbearable. I always want to see if I have a chance to do something about it. Ignoring really doesn't make it disappear.

*"Time has a wonderful way of showing us what really matters."*

— MARGARET PETERS

# A PRIVILEGE TO GET OLDER

As I get older my birthdays are full of gratitude. I feel like I'm grateful I was able to get to this age. Not that I'm very old but some people never even get to see this age. Babies die. Children die. Young people die.

Do I love all the wrinkles on my face or some aches that don't go away? No! But I welcome them anyway. I can breathe, I can walk, I can go to the gym, I can clean my house. These are all blessings in disguise. We may take them for granted. So I pay attention to what's happening around me. There are many people who face illness, some that are fatal. I had a friend who died two years ago and left behind young kids. An amazing mom who was there for her kids any second they needed her. She's gone and even if she had a hard life she would have preferred to be here with her family. It happens. We all know at least one person who died at a young age or has a life threatening disease.

So when my friends complain they're aging or they're not happy to have a birthday that reminds them of their age, I tell them it's a privilege to get older. Not everybody gets the chance to get older, to witness their wisdom, their children's lives, to see their grandchildren or any other meaningful milestone. Yes, your body ages but your soul doesn't need to. You can still feel like a child or like you're in your 20s. I'm lucky to have many friends who don't think old. So next time you feel you're aging and feel unhappy about it, think about all those who lost their lives too early and never got to be old, and just be grateful.

*"Try not to become a man of success, but rather try to become a man of value."*

— ALBERT EINSTEIN

# RESISTING THE "BAD" FEELINGS

We love to be happy, joyful, compassionate, brave and helpful. Then we do everything to avoid the feelings of anxiety, fear, loneliness or sadness. By doing that, we deny being human. Being human has both sides of these feelings. We want to run away from them when they hit us hard.

I was someone who wanted to run away from bad feelings. I didn't let myself feel bad for a long time. I thought of it as a waste of my time. I thought savoring every moment meant being happy every moment of every day. So when I couldn't do it, I tried to hide my not-so-great feelings or deny them. I really believed they went somewhere to never come back. I had no idea why I was so uncomfortable feeling angry or sad. I think in many cultures we're not taught how to deal with these feelings and that they're as normal as our good feelings.

If you have a feeling you're not comfortable with causing you discontent, instead of running away from it, stay with it. Accept that it's there and it's part of being human. Acknowledge that many people have felt or are feeling the same thing right now. You're never the first one feeling this way and won't be the last. We think staying with the hard feelings will crack us open or make us feel worse. Yes, at first it may be overwhelming but if you stay with it, you'll realize your own strength. If you stay long enough or practice doing it many times, you'll see that you don't have the same intensity anymore. I understood that feeling your emotions and staying with them is the only way to deal with hardship in life. When you feel bad, you need to recognize it; know that it's there. Then accept it and stay with it. When I say "Stay with the feelings" I mean sitting down and letting emotions flow through you; feel them in your body and observe without judgment. Make time for yourself to feel it. Have a walk or sit in the park or in your yard and feel it in your body. Breathe with it. This is the only way to heal. It doesn't go anywhere when you deny it. Avoiding these feelings is like trying to avoid the sun. It's already there. We are mostly inclined to *think* our way around things instead of *feel* our way through them. The only way to freedom and peace is to let them flow through us.

I think it's important for our children to know life brings good and bad feelings so they don't struggle with it and resist the bad feelings when they come. There's no smooth ride and only good feelings all the time reserved for anyone. It's important to expect bad feelings and know you're not alone; and learn how to feel those feelings completely. Turn toward the feeling, good or bad. Enjoy and cherish the good ones and feel and accept the hard ones.

*"Happiness isn't something ready-made. It comes from your own actions."*

— DALAI LAMA

# More about happiness

I was listening to Shawn Achor who studies and give classes on happiness. I love to read and learn more about the research behind the study of happiness. Now there's a field called positive psychology that studies it. Shawn says everybody has a baseline of happiness and it's different for all of us. He also redefines happiness and says, "It's not about feeling pleasure which is very short lived... Happiness is the joy we feel as we follow our potential." I love that.

I think the most fascinating statistics out of the research is that only 10% of long term happiness is tied to our circumstances, while 90% is based on how we perceive the world. I watched a documentary about happiness called "Happy" a few years ago. It shows how people who are really "poor" in terms of their possessions are a lot happier when compared with people who have everything. It also showed examples of people who had terrible accidents but still felt happy. Also cultures view happiness in various ways. Unlike how we usually think, we don't necessarily get happier when we acquire a lot of money or when our circumstances get better.

# Create a Life You Love

According to Shawn Achor, we're mostly brought up to believe that working hard and being successful will make us happy but he says this belief is broken now. He says being "successful" in the old conventional sense doesn't make us happier but being happier could lead to more success.

He says we can change our happiness level by choice and by practicing actions like exercise, meditation, saying thank you, having a gratefulness practice every morning and writing about a meaningful thing that happened to you in the last 24 hours. He says even a 21-day practice of integrating these into your life (shown through studies) results in higher levels of happiness.

You can read more in his book *Before Happiness* and also listen to his TED talk.

I think it's great to know science can prove we can learn to be happy and that we don't need to depend on our circumstances to achieve that feeling.

*"I'm not what happened to me,
I'm what I choose to become."*

—C. G. Jung

## STOP BEING A VICTIM AND CREATE YOUR LIFE

U nfortunately I grew up in a society where many saw themselves as victims—almost all the time. Many do not want to take responsibility but love to blame. Blame the circumstances, blame the government, blame the parents, blame the teacher, blame the weather. Anything but yourself. I'm coming from an always-victim society. It happens everywhere and I don't mean everybody is like this back there either but it is pretty common.

This is unfortunate when you start to learn more about human beings. When you're a victim you don't need to do anything. You don't take responsibility to take action. Even if you take one or two steps, you'll prove again that you're a victim because there will always be something that doesn't go according to plan and you can blame anything but yourself for not reaching your goal. You'll always prove yourself right.

Although this looks like the easy way out, we don't always realize the impact. You'll feel powerless when you stay in this victim space. Everything happens *to you*. You feel sorry for yourself. You have no control over your life. You're only reacting to life.

This is depressing. When I see people who are victims of their circumstances, I know they won't have an extraordinary life. They don't see how they can make a difference, how they can create their own lives. They prefer to be lazy and they give up everything. When something bad happens they ask WHY ME? It's their victim mentality. They don't see the choices they have when something bad happens to them. (And something bad happens to all of us.)

I'm glad there's more accountability and more awareness in the society I live in now. Many people know how to take the responsibility for their actions and they don't blame everyone and everything. They're not stuck playing the "It's all my parents' fault" game. Has anyone gone to a therapist and not talk about their parents? It's true our caretakers have the deepest influence on us. Therapy might be necessary to understand why we behave in certain ways. But it's to understand, not to blame. Otherwise everyone would have a problem with their parents. Because no matter what your parents do, even if they were perfect people (who never existed), you'll always find something that impacted you. Even if they said nothing wrong, as children we can make one look mean something and create a story subconsciously. So there's really no point in making our parents wrong. As long as we have parents and caregivers—which we all do—we'll have issues growing up. This is inevitable. Our children have us as parents too. Every generation will know how to do parenting better with the advances in science which means every generation can blame the one before for not doing the best parenting. But they did not know better.

I've met so many people who had terrible things happen to them but they still created powerful lives never falling into the victim trap. They recognized the misfortune but they decided it wasn't going to shape their lives. They know how not to identify themselves with the circumstance no matter how grim it seemed at the time. I've seen people with severe disabilities, who faced unbelievable abuse but still lived amazing lives. They chose to create their lives instead of playing the victim; they saw their own power. Nelson Mandela was a perfect example of this. The government couldn't crush his soul or change what he believed even after 27 years in prison. This is how astonishing the human spirit can be.

We all possess this power and the freedom to choose what to do, who to be no matter what happens to us. I'd rather choose to live a good life and create the life I want instead of playing the victim, feeling weak and sorry for myself. Take a look at where you play victim in your life, and choose to create your life instead!

*"Tear off the mask. Your face is glorious."*

— R<small>UMI</small>

# BETTER AND MORE AUTHENTIC LIFE

I've been reading, listening to CDs and watching TV shows for over 10+ years to see if there are better ways to live a more authentic, more fulfilling life. I feel like I'm at that place where it's easier to see the common denominator in all the things I've read.

Everything starts with the mind and most importantly what you feed your mind, what you say to yourself. It seems like the only way to be happy with who you are and feel successful—which means being happy and fulfilled in all areas of your life—is to be authentic. Do your best to be yourself and live in the present moment. What you've been told when you were growing up doesn't define you. You need to find yourself; your true self which has all the answers for your happiness. When you're authentic with yourself you do the things you love to do and follow your passion and dreams—you become a happy soul.

Whatever book I read, whatever show I watch or whatever CD I listen to about changing your life for the better always starts and ends with you. Nothing external changes that. If you're one of the lucky ones who was authentic when you were growing up then this is easy for you. And that's where all of us need to be. We need to change the programming of our subconscious. If you feel stuck or unhappy or unfulfilled it's because you're not living the real you. You see yourself as you were told to be. You follow rules others laid on you You're not free. But as soon as what others have told you doesn't matter, you become closer to the person you were meant to be.

It would be wonderful if we all took time to rest and relax in this crazy world we live in. We need to take time to be alone and connected to our source. We want to stop believing that we need to be thinking every moment of the day. We would love to stop the chatter in our mind, even if it's for a few seconds a day. Make these few changes to bring you to the only reality which is this present moment. Only by practicing being in the moment and focusing on what we do will all of humanity get to a better place—and lead more authentic lives.

We all need to learn how to slow down and take a break so we can realize who we are and where we are on our life's journey.

The teachings of yoga, meditation, Pilates and such concentrate on the same issues. We need to bring the mind and body together in a seamless way. Our energy wants to smoothly run in our bodies. In meditation the purpose is to stop that the continual thinking and come to the present moment to be connected to ourselves and everything around us. Yoga also brings the attention to the moment and provides physical and mental relaxation. I don't think it surprising to see so many people doing these ancient eastern teachings. We lead cluttered, busy lives; having material things don't always make us happy. We all look for some place to feel free and relaxed and to slow down. We just forgot how to slow down in our life. I think this is why so many people are interested in these eastern teachings. No matter where we are in our life let's take some time to breathe and relax! Your authentic self is in there waiting for you in peace.

*"Perspective is as simple as answering this question: If I had 5 months to live would I experience this problem differently?"*

— SHANNON L. ALDER

# Doing things that matter

When you hear about somebody who's really sick or watch a movie where somebody is going to die and comes to understand the preciousness of life, do you also decide to live your life differently from that moment on? Do you say you'll understand the value of every moment of your life before you face death and promise yourself you won't sway again from this truth?

Do we always need to have a bad experience to believe we need to live a meaningful life being true to who we are? Aren't others' experiences and stories good enough to learn from it? Why can't we use others' advice and recommendations knowing how much suffering they had to go through to learn a valuable lesson? This is my goal. I don't want to wait until something tragic happens to me to live my life to the fullest. Yes, as we age we understand this more and remember it more because we see more people getting sick or dying around us. Can we learn what matters the most before we get to that hard place or have a disease? Yes we can. We need some practice to make this happen but it is possible.

# Doing things that matter

When we close our eyes and focus on the moment we usually don't have anything wrong at the moment. What we worry about is either in the past which we can't change or the future which we can't predict. Of course we all have times we need to grieve too. All we can do is our best and have faith that the Universe will work its miracles. We need to cherish every moment and when we catch ourselves worrying we need to stop and think about whether we have any problems that very second. The answer will most likely be no. Then take a deep breath and have faith that things will work out. If it feels like it won't then you have something to learn from the experience. Worrying never helps. I tried it on many occasions (ha!) and it never worked, not even one time.

Make a list of things that make you happy. Hang it in front of your desk or mirror. Do them as often as you can. Tell the people you love how you feel about them. One thing I see when people lose a loved one is the fact that they don't only feel bad to never see that person again but all the things that they never told to him or her. We don't know how long we will live so don't delay sharing your feelings. Don't assume they already know it. Don't delay what you want to do with your life. See if what comes up are excuses or if there is a way around them.

We shouldn't wait until we have a bad experience to enjoy every moment. It's not easy at first but as with everything else with practice we can build this inner muscle. We are all here to do things that matter to us.

*"It takes as much energy to wish as it does to plan."*

— ELEANOR ROOSEVELT

## ENERGY FROM PEOPLE

The personality test from the Myers-Briggs Type Indicator has a unique definition for extravert and introvert. It shows where you get your energy from. Do you get your energy by being around people or by being by yourself? It has nothing to do with being social or not.

I get my energy from people although I love my "me" time and need that as well. As long as I'm with positive people I get recharged and feel better about my life. Even at times when I feel I want to stay at home and I have plans, I still push myself to go and meet people—and at the end I always feel better.

Some people need to be alone to restore their energy. And some need to balance these two. It's good to know where you stand so you don't force yourself in a way that doesn't work for you. It's important to feel energetic to accomplish what you want and it's good to know how you receive and store this energy you need. It's also helpful to know about this in a work environment so people who need to have the space to restore their energy have the opportunity to do that.

Do the Myers-Briggs test (www.myersbriggs.org) if you get a chance and act according to who you are. Spend time with people or by yourself to get recharged!

*"When you look at a person,*
*any person, remember that*
*everyone has a story.*
*Everyone has gone through*
*something that has changed them."*

— ANONYMOUS

# Everybody has a story
# worth telling

I've always loved to read about and listen to famous and influential people's stories. I got inspired by them. I didn't realize until my 30s that everybody has a story worth telling. We usually find our stories to be not so important or too insignificant to mention. If anybody approached you and wanted you to tell your story most of you would probably be embarrassed or say you have nothing to tell.

But everybody does have a compelling story. Because everyone is unique. No two people's stories are the same even with twins. We experience life in different ways from the day we were born. We come here with a certain number of genes and personalities. Yes, we learn more and change as we grow up but we're always unique and special in our way. We all have experiences that change us.

Believe in your story and think about it. Write about it. If you own a business definitely share it. People love to hear your story. It will mean something to others. It does not have to make the headlines.

Create a Life You Love

Like Martha Beck says in her book *Finding Your Own North Star*, "Be the hero of your autobiography – not the victim."

*"Successful people maintain a positive focus in life no matter what's going on around them. They stay focused on their past successes rather than their past failures, and on the next action steps they need to take to get them closer to the fulfillment of their goals rather than all the other distractions that life presents to them."*

— JACK CANFIELD

# Focus

Whatever we focus on in life seems to grow larger. If we only see the lack in our lives, it seems like the lack grows; if we see abundance in life, we have more of everything.

So even if it's hard to do, even when times are tough, think of all you have in your life and imagine how you're going to receive what you don't have now. If you constantly worry for the love or money you lack, you won't be open to receive them even when they're in front of you. Maybe you have a belief that you can't have it all or you don't deserve it. These are limitations you don't even know you acquired since childhood. We sometimes never question them and sadly we believe them to be true. That inhibits us from getting what we want out of life. Look at people who do the things they love and also get all they want. They got rid of those limiting beliefs or never had them. They were raised to believe they can do it all and have it all. That's why they grabbed every opportunity to get themselves there. When you believe you can't have it or don't deserve it you won't see it even when the opportunity knocks on the door. We get blinded when we believe only "others" can have it. Or we have a fear that we'll fail. We never take the challenge and when we don't take it we can't have all we want from life and have a fulfilled life.

It hit me when I finally believed all those nicely worded bookmarks and signs you can hang in your home and those encouraging cards that were giving the real secrets to happiness. Then I reviewed my life and realized everything I believe I can achieve has happened. Everything. When I was able to believe in myself and in my dream, all of it came true.

Now I'm trying to realize all my dreams, believing that the Universe is there to show me the way. I'm getting rid of my fears one by one. How surprised I was to hear years ago in a coaching class that people are also afraid of being successful too! It made no sense to me at the moment but now I know it's true. I've heard numerous stories already from those who couldn't lose weight because they realized they don't like the attention when they get thin and attractive. Or from those who never found the love they sought for years because it also brought a conflict that they might lose their independence. So pay attention to what you want (and what you focus your attention on) and how you may be standing in your own way. I'm still working on it, believe me. I found my own reasons of not writing this book and great reasons to procrastinate for a long time—and then I had to dig deep down.

It's truly amazing what we do to ourselves. It never made any sense to me when I heard this for the first time but now I know for certain that it's hard to get rid of our old beliefs and live the life we want to live. But once we do it it's the most liberating fulfilling feeling. So make sure you focus on the right things in your life: what you have and what you want!

*"The happiest people don't have the best of everything; they just make the best of everything."*

—Anonymous

# Happy

As I get older I feel like happiness is a privilege and something you can create—not something that was promised to you. As a girl growing up and in my young adult years I thought happiness was promised to me and everything would go according to plan and smoothly. I sometimes go back and question how I got to believe that? Who gave me this illusion? Where and when did I start to believe this? Does it start when we were a child and stay with us?

I was surprised when I was leaving my son for the first time at a sleep-away camp. It was a basketball camp and the coach was telling my son and all other boys aged 8-12 how life is a roller coaster. "There will be good days and bad days" he told them. This sentence shocked me; probably because I came from a culture where difficult things are kept away from children. I don't think I ever told my son about this. I don't think I was so realistic about life like that. I wanted him to see the good things in life and emphasized the good much more than the bad.

Maybe because that's how I grew up getting this false impression that everything will be great! Well I'm lucky. Yes compared to millions of people I'm lucky. But that doesn't mean there are no bumps or disappointments or sorrow on the way. I'm even surprised with the little bumps I had on the way. I was waiting for a constant happiness ride and I used to stress myself out because I was having a bad day or even a bad hour! That was a waste of my life!

Now I cherish my happy days, hours or even minutes. I know anything can change any second. I want to be conscious of each moment of my life, my family, my loved ones; everything I've experienced so far and everything I've been fortunate enough to own!

Now I know the real value of life; sadness is part of life as much as happiness!

When I send my wishes for the New Year to family and friends it seems unreal to say, "I wish you happiness all the time." I want to say, "I wish more happy days than sad ones."

So I know how great it is to feel happy and I cherish every moment! I wish all of you many many happy hours, days and years too!! Learn what it means for you to be happy and pursue that!

*"For after all, the best thing one can do when it's raining is let it rain."*

— HENRY WADSWORTH LONGFELLOW

# Acceptance

R ecently I feel like I finally learned something really big. I learned not to spend all my time worrying about a situation I'm in for weeks, days or months. Instead I'll accept *what is* first and then stay still with the feeling. This is the only way to move forward and take the right steps to resolve the situation. Any decisions we take before we've reached this acceptance level will be made out of fear and may not be the best thing for us. I didn't understand it until I practiced it; it surely felt good.

I've tried the other way, worrying about what might happen next and all the possible terrible outcomes and resisting the situation like "it shouldn't have happened to me" for many years. Believe me, it drains you and slowly kills you. It makes you miserable and you become a negative unbearable person; it doesn't work for your good at all. You don't get anywhere and just stay with your own suffering; it sucks up all your energy.

Observing the reality, accepting the truth and taking steps to move forward feels so much better than feeling like a victim. The most important thing I learned is to stop resisting what is! It is what it is already. If you're sick, if you lost your job, if you can't pay the rent—they're all hard situations to be in. Nobody will take it lightly, whatever the situation is; you're the one living it and it is hard. But resisting isn't the answer. Acceptance is.

You have the right to be sad, angry or frustrated. Feel them. Grieve. What you don't want though is to stay there forever and you don't want to resist it. You're living this moment and you can't change what is now. So the best way is to accept the situation first and then start to think what you can do to change it—if you can. Next make a decision to change your attitude or make changes to resolve the problem. Being proactive and taking some steps makes you feel so much better. You have no power when you resist and when you complain about what's already happening. Yes, we all deserve to vent a little but the sooner we get out of that mood, the better life gets for us.

I really want to believe I understand this because it feels much better and peaceful and I can tell I'm not making myself sick—worrying, resisting and denying. In other words, not accepting!

Life is a constant struggle to find out more about yourself, about living your best life and healing your past wounds. But it's certainly worth it! Accept what is and move on from there.

*"When I was 5 years old, my mother always told me that happiness was the key to life. When I went to school, they asked me what I wanted to when I grew up. I wrote down 'happy.' They told me I didn't understand the assignment, I told them they didn't understand life."*

— JOHN LENNON

## SMALL THINGS IN LIFE

Another piece of wisdom I've learned as I get older is that happiness is momentary. We can make the most of happiness by being aware of it when we feel happy. That exciting peak does not always last too long though. Overall, I'm a happy person and I'm lucky to be this way.

Sometimes you feel good for hours, days, weeks or months but there's also some small and big struggles in life. One small thing can get you down and derail your happiness. As you understand more about this, you can count your happy days and be blessed to have them. You accept when you're not that happy; you accept life with its ups and downs. If you only want ups you're on the wrong planet.

I consider myself lucky to get great pleasure out of small things in life. A simple act of thoughtfulness, one phone call, feeling peaceful while I take a walk, being warm at our house on a rainy day, having a good laugh with my husband while sipping our tea at night, seeing that joyful look of my 10-year old puppy, seeing my son play his guitar—these are just some of the small things that can make me very happy. Life can be tough sometimes and for many people it's easier to focus on what goes wrong or what we lack or what

224

we want next. What we need to learn is to find pleasure in the small things and make the most out of those happy moments. And always count our blessings.

*"Don't get so caught up on the daily grind that you never find time to enjoy yourself."*

— Anonymous

# ME TIME

I need "Me" time to find myself, to live my life, to do the things I love to do. It rejuvenates me, it makes me happy, it makes me feel free.

Today I had a wonderful day. First I woke up to a rainy day; I miss the rain. I went out to our backyard and smelled the rain, the soil, the greenery.

Later, I spent hours (although I had the temptation, I didn't even look at my watch) in the bookstore. It was perfect. I found the books I wanted to buy; I touched them, felt their energy and was happy that I'd be leaving the store with them. Then I took some magazines, bought a cup of coffee and sat down on a comfortable leather chair. It was quiet and peaceful.

Eager to read my new books I went home soon. I took my son to lunch and had a nice chat with him. Then I curled up with my book on our sofa in the living room. As soon as I finished the first book (it was a short one) I started reading another one of my new books. When I needed a break, I took Romeo (my beloved Labrador Retriever) for a walk with my son around the block on a wonderful cloudy afternoon.

I came back and read some more. I made myself a cup of tea, curled up in the living room and read my book. It was perfect.

The book took me to a place I want to go in the future. It took me back to our trip last summer. It made me want to go even more. Maybe that's why I got this book. It took me to this faraway place that I love. I love books that take me somewhere else. I love books that allow me to be part of other people's lives. I love books because I learn so much.

This was my version of my ME time. Find yours. It feeds your soul. It's not selfish. We all need ME time.

*"A person who never made a mistake never tried anything new."*

— ALBERT EINSTEIN

# MISTAKES

Do you allow yourself to make mistakes? Do you beat yourself up when you do? I would say no and yes to these questions respectively—until recently.

Thinking backwards now I must have grown up with high expectations of myself. I have wonderful parents who raised me well and I don't think I took what was expected of me as a big pressure at the time. I don't think they ever wanted me to be the top of my class but obviously they wanted me to go to one of the best high schools in Turkey, be successful and not fail in any of my classes—and also work hard enough to get into one of the best colleges. My parents wanted the best for me and my brother to have the best future and they invested a lot for our education. Failing was obviously not an option. And we didn't. I was in the top 1% of all applicants to attend one of the best colleges. I had to achieve what was put in front of me with no questions asked.

I think to be raised like that and coming from a family with many great achievements makes you think you should never fail. At work or at life. Live your life with no failure and with a fear of making mistakes. I'm finding out that it was a lot to ask from me and it was unrealistic.

# Mistakes

I guess being surrounded by people just like me I never realized I was being too tough on myself until I came to the U.S. and met my new American friend. She kept telling me how hard I am on myself and I never understood what she meant by that. I probably still don't get it entirely but I know more now than I did when I first heard it.

Yes, I realized I did everything I could not to make mistakes. I judged myself harshly when I did make mistakes.

Years later I met people at work who got to know me well pretty fast. I learned a lot about myself from them. I heard the same from my bosses: "You're too hard on yourself." When I heard it from a few other people, I knew I had to dig deeper in myself to find out more. People who knew me well were telling me the same thing. We have to pay attention when something is repeated so many times. The first time I heard someone telling me that "it's okay to make mistakes", I was 38. That was a light bulb moment for me. It's still amazing how I never heard that from anybody until I was 38! And then this became addictive; I had just needed somebody to tell me this. I was feeling a big relief. It had a healing power on me. Is it really okay to make mistakes? Nothing will happen? Will I still be the same person? Then I realized I didn't need anybody to say that to me; I just needed to say that to myself! I never did that before. I only judged myself.

I started practicing to feel okay with small mistakes. Little things like breaking something in the kitchen or forgetting to call a friend. I had to tell myself, "It's okay, you're fine, it's going to be okay" to make sure I was okay with my mistakes. I also listened to many people who I considered to be successful, people I admired and I heard dozens of times how making mistakes and facing failure is part of the journey and how it's impossible to live otherwise. I also realized that if you want to *avoid* making mistakes there's a high cost as well. You'll never try big things, you'll never take risks and you'll stay small. You'll also lose your connection with people you care about because you feel bad about yourself when you make mistakes. Instead of sharing your humanity and being vulnerable with your mistake, you hide some part of you. Having learned all of this, I'm much kinder to myself. It's still tough sometimes but I know this is the only way to chase my best life, expecting there will be mistakes and failures on the way but never giving up. I'll keep on telling myself it's okay! Is it okay for you to make mistakes?

*"Realize deeply that the present moment is all you have. Make the NOW the primary focus of your life."*

— ECKHART TOLLE

# OUR CLUTTERED MIND

I've learned to think all my life. Thinking was one of the best things I could do.

Then I learned that we have to stop thinking so much all the time. We need to have some space between the thousands of thoughts in our minds.

You know how I got to learn this? Somebody I met for the first time told me I needed to read the book *The Power of Now* by Eckhart Tolle. At first I didn't pay too much attention but when two more people told me the same I decided I should buy and read it. It seems like a simple concept but it's hard to do.

It is to stay focused in the present moment and have your mind cleared from thoughts about the past and the future. You have to start by becoming aware of all the talk you have going on in your mind. Once you become aware of and start paying attention to it you'll know how much of is it going on. For most of us it's non-stop!

What's recommended in the book is to concentrate on your breathing even if it's for seconds at first; then to stop thinking and stay in the moment. It's challenging to do it for someone like me who believed thinking non-stop served me better! Now I'm totally convinced it doesn't. I love that we have meditation and yoga and eastern teachings that help us stop the clutter and enjoy the silence of our minds to get to a healthier more spiritual place. The more I do this the more I can feel how much better it is for my soul and my physical being. My body isn't as tensed and it gets a break when I take time to shut off my mind. I feel much better as soon as I experience the now moment and realize most of my worries are for the future. Worry is killing our precious moments, being concerned about all the things that may never happen!

It was such a different mindset for me to accept this because one needs to be mindless and I never thought it would be right not to use my mind or to be so relaxed that I could shut my thoughts off!

When you practice enough, read about the teachings and get convinced as to why we all need to quiet our cluttered minds, you'll start to see the benefits. It was one of the hardest things to change in me but I think it was the most necessary one too! Results: more peace, joy and connection.

*"If we cannot now end our differences, at least we can help make the world safe for diversity."*

— JOHN F. KENNEDY

## Our differences

I love the differences between humans. We need to be different. I can't imagine wanting to be a software engineer while the engineer can't imagine talking to customers all day. Some people get passionate about teaching while others love to take care of flowers. Some love to write, some love to teach. Who would do the other jobs if we all were the same and liked the same things? It would be so boring.

I guess some of us grow up thinking we should be the same, think the same, feel the same as everyone else. We think everybody is like our parents or our siblings. As we grow up, we see differently. (It's that time when we start judging our parents after visiting our friends' houses. Hmm…maybe they shouldn't have been so strict with me since George's parents are much more accommodating.) At the same time we have a tendency to resist change. We want the familiar we want the known even if it's not the best for us. We have that comfort zone we don't want to leave even if it doesn't serve us well. (Isn't that the reason we find the wrong person who continues to treat us as others did in our childhood?)

We want our patterns; we don't want change. We want our spouses to act like us, be like us.

And if we really want happiness for ourselves as well as people around us, we start to question, we start to learn, we start to understand the differences and the beautiful thing that happens when we ACCEPT the differences. We learn that the differences between us and our spouses, parents, children, friends and colleagues are what make life fun and exciting.

That's so much more refreshing than denying the differences, resisting them or trying to change everyone to think, feel or act like we do. We learn to agree to disagree.

It's not always easy to accept others' differences, but when we can do it and respect the perspective of others, it makes for wonders in this world. I believe all of us are needed in this world along with the beauty that comes from our differences.

*There is a cure for being overwhelmed: Just take a few breaks for silent time during your day and make a shorter to-do-list. Everything is going to be okay.*

— OZLEM BROOKE EROL

# Overwhelmed

This is the disease of these last decades, if not before. As we have more means to make life move faster, life get more hectic and chaotic. As we have more ways to make life easier, our lives get more complicated. We never seem to have enough time and most of us are overwhelmed. We just have too much to do. We feel like we never catch up. There's always more to do, there are always lists that get longer and longer and we feel like we can never do enough.

I watched a TV show about overwhelmed mothers and women. There were so many examples of mothers who are feeling overwhelmed. They all thought they couldn't live up to the definition of being a good mother. Most wanted to be everything: a good mother, good employee, good wife, good friend, etc.—and they're all exhausted. They never seem to get close to their goal. Then they feel terrible for not being there yet. They feel terrible because they forget important things about their children. They feel bad when there are mistakes made. Nobody is in the moment—they're always three steps ahead in their mind. With no focus on the things they're doing now there are many things forgotten, many things not done right and lots of exhaustion.

I can relate to this. And I have only one child. But I know how it feels when you're overwhelmed; how it feels when you can't be the best at everything. How you feel guilty for not being there for someone you love, either your parents, your husband, your son or a friend. I know how it feels to look at all the things you need to do and not know where to start. How it feels to be so tired at the end of the day with a lot of items that didn't get done. How bad it feels when you have a growing list of things to do. How guilty a mom feels when some of those items are related to her child.

Overwhelmed is the disease of the day and we need to cure it by slowing down and questioning the definitions in our minds. What does a good mother mean? What does a good employee mean? What does a good housewife mean before we kill ourselves? We need to learn how to ask for help and how to take time for ourselves so we can do good for others. Let's be realistic about our expectations. Let's understand the difference between what must be done and what we want done. We all know what our children want more than anything is to be with us. Some quality time when we're not thinking about the rest of the list. Even if it's 15 minutes a day just go to their room and listen to what they have to say with your full attention. Let's be good to ourselves and celebrate all the things we can do for our loved ones and stop being a super hero. Being overwhelmed doesn't help anyone. Practice paring your daily list down to the essentials so you can be there for others—and yourself!

*"The people who are crazy enough to think they can change the world are the ones who do."*

— STEVE JOBS

## PEOPLE WHO BRING OUT THE BEST IN US

Sometimes we meet people who bring out the best in us. Sometimes it works both ways which is even better. You both bring the best in each other. When someone compliments you, it may sound unreal to you. But that new person in your life can see the real you that you've become; that person can see you better than you see yourself. You still see the person with the baggage; you still see the person with the mistakes of the past.

The new person in your life sees the wonderful you, the wonderful person you turned out to be, that person you worked so hard to be. That's why she knows you only deserve the best while you still have a hard time believing it yourself. Listen because she's right.

Surround yourself with people who support you, who give you positive energy, who believe in you. Sometimes we need people who believe in us more than we believe in ourselves.

Think about the people who are there for you, who see the best in you and keep them in your life. Share your dreams with them. They'll help you along the way even when you have self-doubt. If you don't have anyone in your life who brings out the best in you, find someone and bring out the best in them.

*"Pets may be part of your life but you are their whole life."*

— Anonymous

## Our pets

I love my dog... it's such a different form of love that I haven't experienced before. He's so sweet and so innocent, he loves me unconditionally. It's unbelievable to me. Dogs are man's (and woman's) best friend for a reason. I love my dog Romeo. He's such a big part of my life. He brings me joy, he brings me happiness and lot of loyal love.

I can show my love to him in many ways and he loves it all. He brings me to the moment.

If people can be like the pets, so in the moment, so loyal, so innocent, so unconditional in their love so happy with little things—we'd be a much healthier planet.

Animals have a soul like we do and I'm delighted to have a living beautiful being in our house. Make the best out of your time with your great animal companions.

*"If you can dream it, you can do it."*

— Walt Disney

# Results and the process

Life is all about the journey. Because where you want to be is a moving target and whatever milestone you hit there's always another goal to achieve. So we need to enjoy the journey.

At the same time when you want something and don't necessarily like all the steps of that journey, it helps to concentrate on your goal. Visualize it as if you've achieved it all and you're there now. Pay attention to how you feel. It might still be a moving target but stay in the feeling of being there already.

If you concentrate on the process to get there it's not always easy. I'll give you my example of trying to lose weight years ago. It's one of those things I believed I could do against everything my grandma said. She used to tell me I could never be thin. But I didn't believe her.

When I was on a diet I was consistently thinking of myself fitting in a size 2 skirt, looking healthy and thin. I was even dreaming of people telling me how fit I looked. Every time I hit the gym or said no to a delicious dessert all I was thinking of was that image of me. That gave me the strength and the will to do what I needed to do. If I focused on all the dragging I had to do to be at the gym even on days I didn't want to go or all the wonderful food I was missing every single day, I don't think I would have made it. And I got there! Everything and even more happened than what I dreamed of. I lost the weight and haven't gained it back for 25 years. Because I also made a promise to myself that I wouldn't gain weight again and healthy eating would be my lifestyle, not part of a temporary diet plan. I stuck to it.

This mindset could apply to finishing school, pursuing your dream of building your business, working out for a marathon or anything that's important to you. The process is sometimes hard or complex but if you keep focused on your goal and dream about it, you can achieve anything you like.

When I have a goal and it's a long journey I visualize what I'll get at the end and how I'll feel. When the process is too overwhelming I divide it into little pieces and look at my daily and weekly progress instead of stressing about the whole process. I break it down to little doable steps.

Try it and you'll see that the process gets easier when you keep in mind *why* you're doing it and how you'll feel at the end!!

*"Just watch this moment, without trying to change it at all. What is happening? What do you feel? What do you see? What do you hear?"*

— JON KABAT-ZINN

# MINDFULNESS

Another great practice that's spreading in popularity in the last 10 years is mindfulness. As Jon Kabat-Zinn defines it, "Mindfulness is the awareness that emerges through paying attention on purpose, in the present moment, and non-judgmentally to the unfolding of experience moment to moment."

I learned and read about mindfulness years ago when I read in a magazine that Jon Kabat-Zinn, who's a Professor of Medicine Emeritus, created the Stress Reduction Clinic and the Center for Mindfulness in Medicine, Health Care, and Society at the University of Massachusetts Medical School. I read about the impact this practice had on many patients who were going through difficult health problems. He studied the effects of mindfulness-based stress reduction (MBSR) on numerous patients and saw positive results. It certainly wasn't only for the sick but also for anybody who wanted to reduce their stress levels. Having tried meditation, I thought this was similar and it had scientific proof behind it. So I got the audio tapes and followed his plan for eight weeks practicing mindfulness. It certainly made me feel calmer and reduced my anxiety tremendously.

A few years after I read about mindfulness, one of the best scientific institutions, University of California San Diego, opened its Mindfulness Center and started the MBSR and Mindful Self-Compassion classes. So I signed up. Now there are many schools, hospitals and organizations getting engaged with mindfulness practices and seeing the benefits.

Examples of mindfulness are practicing awareness of the smallest things you do, like brushing your teeth, every step you take while you walk, tasting every bite of the food you eat, driving knowing where you are, listening to someone without thinking what you're going to say next, feeling your sadness—so basically focusing only on what you're doing right now in this moment without judgment.

You can try this any time you remember during the day by getting into the moment and observing what you're doing. Once you start doing this you'll realize how many times your mind wanders and how you're almost never present. We're usually in the past or the future. We're missing out on our own experiences. The classic example is arriving at work not remembering how we got there. We're on auto-pilot mode. I'm sure you know what I mean.

You can look online to find out more about how MBSR scientifically works to make patients feel better and how we can all benefit no matter where we are in our lives. See what you can be mindful of throughout the day.

*"The spiritual journey is individual, highly personal. It can't be organized or regulated. It isn't true that everyone should follow one path. Listen to your own truth."*

— RAM DASS

# Spirituality

Anytime you ask your inner guidance about anything besides your basic instincts like eating, sleeping and start to ask who you really are, why you came to this earth, what's your life purpose—all of that is your spirituality.

There's more to life than doing our daily routine tasks. We hopefully are also fulfilling our life purpose and doing something for us as well as for oneness and for the good of a bigger world than ourselves.

A person doesn't need to be religious to feel spiritual. It's about being present, connected and being really alive. It's more than our five senses. We're becoming more multisensory as Gary Zukav explains in his book *Seat of The Soul*.

When I started reading all these personal growth and spiritual books, although I enjoyed reading them and understood most of the messages in my daily life, it also made me feel helpless or weak when I couldn't implement the methods they offered to obtain greater growth.

At first I felt like I had to get rid of all the bad traits I inherited from my past until I read Eckhart Tolle's *New Earth*.

# Spirituality

In it, he says to be present as many times as possible during the day; he wants you to be aware of your thoughts and your noisy mind. Aware only. Not to fix things or change things or expect to change it all. It's not to judge either. Just accept they're there. That awareness brings you to the present and you can watch your ego and know it's not you.

I think being spiritual feeds our soul and gets us aligned with who we really are. When our life and our souls match we feel a great sense of peace; everything flows. We all have those moments when we don't keep track of time and hours pass by and we feel connected and at peace. That happens when we're doing what we're supposed to do. Spirituality taught a lot to me. Like Dalai Lama says in his books and his speeches, it's beautiful when spirituality co-exists with science. What is spirituality to you?

*"There is no better test of a man's integrity than his behavior when he is wrong.".*

— MARVIN WILLIANS

# Integrity

One of the core values I was brought up with was integrity. That meant to do what I promised to do and walk the talk. What I promised always mattered to me. I wanted people to trust me when I made a promise. I would be on time; I would do what I was told to do; I would finish my tasks at work; I bought the toy I promised my son; I visited my parents at the time I told them; I sent the proposal on time to my clients. I always felt good keeping my word and being in integrity with my values.

I realized I didn't promise anything unless I was 100% sure I would deliver it. If not I would either not say anything or at the most I would say, "I'll try." I understood years later at a Landmark Seminar (make sure you attend Forum if you're close to any Landmark education center) that this also made me stay small. Because I didn't want to break any of my promises or fail in what I said I'd do, I only said my full YES to projects I was sure to complete.

I didn't know at the time that you can give your word and do your best but sometimes things may not work out. Yet you always have a chance to restore your integrity. If you promised to be somewhere at a certain time and even if you did your best to keep your word but something else came up, you can pick up the phone and say you won't be able to make it. If you do this all the time obviously it's not integrity. If you keep 90% of your promises and this happens only once in a while then it doesn't mean you lack integrity. If you've done something wrong you feel bad about, you can apologize to the person affected by your actions. You can admit you did something wrong.

So although your word is your promise and it's important to keep it, you can also commit to something huge, do your best and be okay if it couldn't be completed. If you always say, "I'll try" it means you don't have anything at stake. You can stray away any time so you don't feel bad when you don't do it. When you're playing a big game you want all your skin in the game. You can't win it with half a heart. That's what my seminar leader told me. I was shocked to hear it but he was right; you'll stay small if you only make promises that you're 100% sure you'll fulfill.

Sometimes you need to take a leap of faith and say YES to something you haven't even figured out how to do, but when you do it with your full heart, magic can happen. You can be dedicated to run a full marathon, you can launch an international business, you can start a big family, you can move to another country. You do your best, stay on the path and keep your word to yourself. You're still in integrity as long as you communicate what you couldn't finish while doing your best.

*Stillness is one of your
safest places to be.*

— OZLEM BROOKE EROL

## Stillness

One of the hardest things I had to learn was to be able to sit still and relax. I was raised to believe this was inefficiency and unproductiveness which wasn't welcome in our house. To this day I see my father doing something almost every minute of his waking hours. I love him for that and it's who he is but I inherited this without questioning it, which didn't always serve me well.

One day I realized this made me tired and overwhelmed. It became my disease. I always had too much on my mind and too much on my to-do list and the opposite wasn't an option. I had to be busy and productive all the time, otherwise? I didn't know; I suppose that would mean I wasn't good enough, I wasn't a good person, I wasn't productive, I wasn't successful—just lazy. I didn't ever think there was another option. I was on the go overwhelming myself all the time. I never seemed to have enough time, never felt good when I achieved anything because I had much more to do. This started making me dissatisfied and unhappy.

My husband gave me a good insight. He observed me and what I said to myself. He realized I used "I must" in front of almost everything I did. He made me realize the difference between the things I have to do and the things I want to do. It was a big light bulb moment for me. He was so right. I then noticed how much pressure those words had on me. I had to do this, I had to do that and when I don't have enough time on my hands, how did I feel? Like I failed myself. I was in this cycle for so long that I never noticed it. Amazing how our brain is programmed from childhood. I realized I was trying to be like my dad who was a big influence on me growing up. I didn't see any other way. With the disease-to-please-your-parents instinct, I was doing the same to be that productive, valuable, successful, hard-working person.

When I started paying attention to what I said to myself I got better and better at reducing the number of things I planned for a day and stopped feeling bad. I also started taking a deep breath from time to time. I gave permission to myself to take time off and do nothing. I gave myself permission to do three things instead of trying to do 13 on a given day and feeling like a failure at the end. I started having reasonable to-do lists. I stopped beating myself up if I had time only to do three instead of 13. What a relief!

It was not only cutting my list down but also having the new knowledge that I learned about being in stillness and how important it is for my well-being. Having too much clutter in my mind and too many things to do in one day isn't the best thing for my mind and spiritual being. I feel so much more relaxed and happy with myself now that I'm taking the time to meditate to do nothing but enjoy the silence and not feel guilty about it. Stillness, breathing gives us a space between our thoughts. Even a few seconds of this space is good for our well-being.

Now when I catch my dad saying "I have to…" I remind him those are things he "wants to do", not "have to do" and we laugh, but I guess he's okay with that. Not me! Don't feel bad to sit still and get your mind off your to-do list. You have the right to feel tired and not clean the house for that day or to sit and enjoy your book instead of doing the laundry. We all need to find space in our lives to listen to our inner music. It's not easy at first but as in everything else, as you practice you get better at it. You'll so love the peace that comes from being in stillness.

*"The planet doesn't need more successful people. The planet desperately needs more peacemakers, healer, restorers, storytellers and lovers of all kinds."*

— DALAI LAMA

# Success

Do you know how you define success? Most of us do it through the eyes of our parents or caregivers. Some of us do it through the eyes of the society. It's important to make the definition right for ourselves and what we value. We can be very successful by some definitions, but if we don't feel fulfilled is it really success for us? I've met and read about thousands of people who've been very successful on the corporate ladder where people envied them for their positions, for the money they were making, their possessions or simply for the way they dressed and where they ate. But I've seen so many of them not feeling happy, feeling lost or feeling like a failure. Isn't that sad? It's like why my mom was worried when I wanted to leave my job at a Fortune 100 company with a good salary and benefits. Yes, it was great in a lot of ways but it wasn't for me. I started to lose myself in my job and that didn't feel good. Every time I felt bad or unhappy others including my mom would remind me how lucky I was to work there and lead the kind of life I had. That was true when you looked at it from the outside. But if you listened to how I felt inside it didn't feel so great at all. I was at one of the top companies, I made money faster than I ever dreamed of, I had great benefits and a good environment with lots of great friends but I was losing myself. What could be more important than my happiness and peace of mind? I tried several times to find my passion elsewhere and I couldn't leave the company for years because it was easier and in my comfort zone to stay. But I finally did it before we moved to the U.S.

I can't say it was easy at first besides all the other changes in my life but when I look back, I know I did the right thing for me. Although looking at my life from the outside I would be considered fortunate and successful in my corporate job, but it didn't feel like success to me at all. Because I wasn't fulfilled, I wasn't doing what I meant to do and it wasn't me.

So define what "success" means to you. Being there for your family, waking up every morning knowing you're doing what you love, going to sleep in peace every night, being a great gardener, doing your creative work, having a balanced life—whatever success is for you. Something that fulfills you, not something you do to impress others or only looks great on paper.

*One of the best outcomes of
coaching is to be aware of our
limited beliefs and overcome
them. With that alone, you can
build a completely different life.*

—OZLEM BROOKE EROL

# Why I love coaching

I've always wanted to do something positive that would affect people's lives, their daily lives. Something that would make their lives better, easier, more fulfilling. I didn't know what it was. There's value you can bring to somebody by being in any profession. That's why we need to find out what that is for ourselves. For me, there had to be more of a connection with the people at a deeper level, something I could offer them that made them happier in their daily lives. That was my calling. That's why I was drawn to coaching even when I didn't know what it was. "Coaching" still brings up different meanings to different people but it's really not that important what the label is. What's important is what it can do for people; I'm absolutely amazed and excited about it.

I've been in this conversation since 2003 and I've been to several trainings, associations and meetings where I got to meet many coaches. As I saw it being practiced right in front of my eyes and having received incredible coaching myself for many years, I fell in love with this business. This was the platform to practice what I believed in. It doesn't matter what it's called; we sometimes get too hung up on the words or the labels. Coaching is believing in the full potential, creativity and greatness in people. I've always believed that since I was a child. I knew nobody was born to be bad; it was the circumstances that made them do bad things. Actually there's really nobody that's "bad". Even the worst criminals have something about them we can be compassionate about. They didn't come here to kill in the first place.

The most amazing coaches I've met are here to change the world for the better; one person at a time, one group or one company at a time. They want to help people see their own greatness and their own power and what makes them special. Also to get rid of the limiting beliefs they've inherited over time. We don't see our own blind spots but it's a lot easier to see it in others. That's why the best coaches also have their own coaches. Since I started coaching there've been a lot of advances in the field and it's been more widely spread in the business world too. Top CEOs and business owners saw the value they get from coaching. Among them are tough guys who you would never think would ask for any kind of help to do their jobs better. Many know this isn't a sign of weakness but actually a strength; to accept that we may not know everything, we can be vulnerable and we need to be kept accountable.

Everybody has their answers buried inside them. Coaches only show them how to access the answers and how to trust themselves and be the person they were meant to be. I'm thrilled to do this work. I'm there for anyone who's willing to live their best life no matter what. I'm willing to be there for people who lost themselves. I'm willing to hold a mirror to their greatness and to their endless potential. I believe in coaches who are changing the world to be a better place. Our world certainly needs this and I love being part of this journey.

*"Best thing you can give
your children is TIME."*

— JD G<small>HAI</small>

# Raising children with more consciousness

Knowing how much impact we have on our children makes me wonder what I did wrong when I raised my son. As I learned about human beings and how to live a better life, in the back of my mind I also thought how this should all be implemented in parenting. It's not easy. I already had my son before I started this journey so if some damage is done, I have to accept that some of that precious time is already over. I also learned there are ways to make it better even for the past. I learned in this journey that we all make mistakes as parents no matter how hard we try to be the best. For the simple fact that we're human. When I went into deeper thoughts of how I might have some negative impact on my son, my husband reminded me it's bound to happen and that there's no way to avoid it. Our son will interpret meanings about our actions, like we all did as we grew up. Most of these meanings are done subconsciously. It doesn't mean we stop trying our best but we had bad days and good days and some of that got reflected on him. We tried our best to stay in open communication. We told him we were sorry when we knew it wasn't his fault. We always kept our promises to build that trust in him and explained the reason behind our decisions.

I even told him how conflicting I may look since I still had the old beliefs of how I should guide him as a parent and all the new things I learned in my journey in a new country. I knew I was sometimes giving conflicting messages, so why not admit it? I tried to get over my ego looking like I knew everything. I didn't. And it should be okay for him when he's a parent to know you don't always have all the answers. You just learn as you go about life and it's okay to say, "I don't know" and "I'm sorry".

I also understood that as a conscious parent, being older or taller didn't give me the right to exercise authority. It only gave me the right to guide him towards who he wants to be. I had lots of moments and days that I couldn't do it and when I dug a little deeper it was always my fear getting in the way. What if he fails? What if he feels disappointed? What if he can't handle it himself? As a mother especially, you always want to create that soft place for them to fall; you don't know what to do with yourself if you let them be and have them fall flat on their face. It's not only about seeing them suffer; it's about not knowing how to handle yourself as a parent that causes the fear. At least in our Turkish culture we're more protective and try to prevent all harm no matter what. But in this country I learned you have to give them the wings to fly (at an early age) and know they can fall but can get up and continue life on their own terms. I learned that we don't give them a chance to learn if we protect them all the time. It's just not realistic though because we may not always be there for them and they have to learn to stand up on their own feet.

I think this was and still is the hardest thing for me to learn: to let go of your grown up child and believe everything will be all right. And be okay if they fail or feel disappointed from time to time. It's their life and they only come through us not for us. We have to let them "be" who they're meant to be and that might be completely different from what we dreamed for them. We can't be selfish to dictate them to do what looks right to us. They need to find it on their own. They're a different person, they're a different generation and they have different dreams.

I'm not saying this is easy at all. It's very difficult and I always tell my son motherhood is a form of sickness and that it doesn't seem to go away either. I believe the right way is to give soft guidance observing their strengths and supporting them. The best thing we can give them is still unconditional love and lots of quality time where we're 100% with them so they can do the same for their own children one day.

*"Rather than getting more spoiled with age, as difficulties pile up, epiphanies of gratitude abound."*

— ALLAIN DE BOTTON

# With age comes more gratitude

I recently went back to Turkey to visit family and friends. One thing I realized was the appreciation and gratitude everyone felt for being healthy. Almost everyone I called answered me with saying, "Thank God we're all okay and healthy." I think as we age we understand how important being healthy is. I remember my younger years and how people older than me always wished for our good health and it meant something, but nothing like what I feel today. I think as we age we start to witness or hear many heart-breaking stories about health. We raise children and we understand how important it is for them to be healthy. My dad always tells me the biggest lottery in this world is to be healthy, since he's a doctor and knows how many organs in our body need to work in harmony to keep us healthy. This is so true. We usually ask, "Why me?" when we get sick but we never question why we're healthy.

When I've been sick for a few days and I'm bored I have this impatience to feel better to go on with my life. Then it makes me feel so grateful that I'm healthy when so many others are diagnosed with illnesses that will affect the rest of their lives or people are born with disabilities who can't function as I do every day. The smallest things taken away from us show us how we take every day granted while we need to remind ourselves how lucky we are every single day.

One thing I know for sure is most of us are more aware of our luck as we age. These days when my plans are interrupted it's a great reminder for me to count my blessings.

I highly recommend having a gratitude journal and a gratitude prayer. I've been doing this for the last five to six years. I practice this daily and it's changed my life. I certainly feel better even in the wake of hardship. I was always falling into the trap of thinking about what I lacked (when I had so much to be grateful for). Not anymore. I do go there occasionally, but I get out of there much faster because of my awareness. I catch myself quickly. I've heard from positive psychologists that people who are the happiest are the ones who are grateful for what they have. So with age and understanding life better, our level of gratitude grows. We can also teach our children gratitude at a much earlier age so that they're happier for a much longer time.

*I leave you with great gratitude that you've picked up this book and read it. I wish you got at least one bit of wisdom out of it that will stay with you to make your life better and happier!*

# ENDING

Wwhat I've learned over my lifetime is that we all strive to be loved and to love. If we have only one person who understands and hears us for who we really are our lives are saved. Unfortunately, we all have a version of "not ____ enough": not good enough, not smart enough, not wealthy enough, not creative enough or the like. If we only knew how powerful we all are and if we use that power to bring the best of us to share with the world, our lives would get a lot better. We all share the same humanity. Everything you think that's wrong with you is true for each one of us. By being vulnerable and sharing our real humanity, we give the chance for everybody around us to do the same. If we know we're never alone in any of our feelings and any of our circumstances, we realize we're very connected. If we choose love instead of fear when we make our decisions, life takes us through a more joyful path. I love this story: just as a caterpillar thinks the world is over, it turns into one of the most beautiful creatures on earth: a butterfly. It's true for us too. When we go through some hard times we should never lose hope; the best part might yet come.

Enjoy your precious journey here. We were never promised a tomorrow so why not make the best out of it when we have this moment? Live a life that matters to you, that means something to you. Make sure you have time to do what you love whatever form and shape it takes. Find a way to do things that you enjoy no matter how hard it looks right now. Every day is so precious. Create and live a life that you LOVE, the BEST version of *your* life!

If some of the concepts and practices here didn't sound right to you today, I understand that. You never know; it may change over time. If I had read some of what I wrote here 20 years ago it wouldn't have made sense to me either. We change, we learn and what we found to be meaningless and odd sometimes gets to make more sense later in life. So give me the benefit of the doubt if you can.

I couldn't include all the wonderful inspiring stories that exemplify what I shared here. To read and listen to these stories and all the inspirational quotes you can always go to my Facebook page www.facebook.com/yourbestlifeinc where I collect them. You can also follow me on www.twitter.com/yourbestlifeinc  or sign up on my website to receive the newsletters at www.yourbestlifeinc.com.

My new journey as I finish this book is to look at the new workplace that is emerging slowly but surely that embraces our strengths and our passion. I believe we are moving into a new business era where finding our purpose, living with

# Ending

our passion and our own priorities, living a life with meaning (instead of selling our soul for our jobs) is going to be crucial. We won't wait until our retirement to do what we love but make it part of our daily lives. We will work and have time to play at the same time. We all know deep in our hearts that we cannot go on being slaves to our jobs to make money for a lot longer. We at least all know our kids will not put up with it. So I choose to be part of the change I want to see in the workplace. I hope we get to have conversations about this topic with you too. I'm in the process of designing my new website in this subject as I'm finishing this book: www.purposeful.business.

*With complete acceptance of where you are now and what you feel about this book, I'm filled with love and gratitude. Thank you!*

*Best,*
*Ozlem Brooke Erol*

# Create a Life You Love

*Thanks to all the café shops, bookstores and libraries in San Diego that inspired me. You provided the best environment for me to write with a cup of hot coffee in my hand.*

Pannikin, Encinitas

Gold Fish Point Café, La Jolla

Java Depot, Solana Beach

Café 976, Pacific Beach

Upstart Crow Bookstore and Coffee House, Seaport Village

Café 1134, Coronado

Bella Vista, La Jolla

Java Earth Café, Pacific Beach

Starbucks, Solana Beach, Rancho Penasquitos, Del Mar

Borders (I miss it a lot)

Barnes & Noble stores everywhere

Encinitas Library

Central Library San Diego